The Autobiograph

Captain Peter Hull

(1942 -)

Chapter 1

In the beginning

I was born in the year 1942. My mother and father lived at Pound Farm, Cholsey, near Wallingford in Oxfordshire. My father and grandfather were tenant farmers who took over the tenancy of Pound Farm from my Uncle Sydney when he moved to a larger farm in Hampshire. My cousin Daphne and I were both born while we lived at Pound Farm.

Pound Farm, Cholsey

My parents were very happy at Pound Farm, but in 1945 they moved to take up the tenancy of Dollars Grove Farm, North Crawley, a much larger farm in Buckinghamshire. It was here that I grew up and all my early memories are of Dollars Grove Farm.

Many people ask why 'Dollars'? The name seems strangely out of place. But looking at some old maps and documents it is probably a corruption of 'Dallows' or 'Hollows' both of which appear to have been used.

E.G. GREAT CRAWLEY MANOR (afterwards Hollowes) was obtained in fee by John Fitz Niel, (fn. 19) either the father, who died about 1289, (fn. 20) or the son, who died about ten years later, leaving as heir his daughter Joan, wife of John son of Richard Handlo.

Dollars Grove Farm was one of a number of tenanted farms belonging to the Crawley Grange Estate which was owned by the Boswell family. At one time it was spelt Dollarsgrove Farm according to the 1900 Ordinance Survey map.

Growing up on a farm is a unique experience. Farm children get caught up in the day to day affairs of the farm, and from an early age they and hurry home from school to find out what has been happening. And if they can, they get stuck in to whatever job is going on at the time. And then of course in later life they look back fondly through rose-tinted spectacles and remember those warm summer evenings spent playing cricket in the field, helping with the harvest or hay-making.

Dollars Grove Farmhouse c.1950

But inevitably the farm, and memories of life on the farm, will become firmly embedded in their heads forever. Ours was a mixed farm with cattle, sheep, pigs, poultry and arable, mostly farmed in the traditional way employing several farm workers.

My father with the cart horses Peggy and Beauty with my sister Judith c. 1949

The village of North Crawley was about 2 miles away. This was where I first went to school and where we did most of our daily shopping because, although a small village, it had a bakery, a small grocer's shop, three pubs, a blacksmith, a saddler & chimney sweep, a post office, a builder, a garage, a district nurse, a village policeman, a church, a chapel, and numerous other individuals who did odd jobs such as decorating, taking in washing or cutting hair. In those days there was also a certain amount of casual work on the farms at busy times such as threshing, harvest or hoeing. The village was quite an active place, but for the most part the people were poor and mostly lived in cottages belonging to the Estate.

*** The Story of Gooby ***

Our farm was situated up East End, which was a collection of farms and cottages about two miles on the east side of the village.

The farms were called – Rookery Farm, Manor Farm, Dollars Grove Farm, Quakers Farm and East End Farm, and there were several farm workers' cottages in small groups along the road. To get there it was necessary to cross 'the ford', and in the winter we were sometimes cut off for days or even weeks if the ford was 'up' due to heavy rains. Nearby one group of cottages contained a small shop run by a woman called Ada Goodman, who lived there on her own except for eleven cats. Because I could not say 'Goodman' when I was a small boy, I used to call her Gooby instead.

Gooby was very old and she was married to Henry Goodman who lived in a cottage at the other end of East End. We used to call him Henry the Ninth. Every day Henry the Ninth would to push his bike up to see Gooby, and then push it all the way back, a distance of about a mile. He never rode the bike, he only pushed it. He and Gooby had not lived together for a long time and occasionally Gooby would threaten to call the village policeman about getting a divorce.

The cottage where Gooby lived and had her shop was at the end of a small terrace. In those days there was no electricity or modern facilities. For water, there was a well at the front. The cottages all had outside loos at the bottom of each garden, and the buckets were emptied by 'Lavender Larry', who came round every week with his horse and cart. The cottage itself had two rooms downstairs and one room upstairs with a landing. Unfortunately, the floor was unsafe upstairs, so Gooby lived downstairs having the shop at the front and living in the back room. She didn't have a bed but slept sitting in a chair fully clothed.

The shop had a passageway through the centre, and on either side there were heaps of tins. On the tins sat the cats. Gooby herself sat in a chair at the back of the shop surrounded by tins and cats, and at her elbow was a jam jar with a pair of scissors in it. These scissors were used for cutting coupons out of peoples' ration books, because in those days food was still rationed. For some time after the WW2 people were only allowed to buy so much of this or that. However, Gooby was very frightened of thunder, and if a storm threatened she would hide the scissors for fear that they would attract the lightening.

Next to the shop there was a lane called 'Ada's Lane, named after her. Often we would see Gooby coming back up the lane pulling a large branch of a tree. She had been 'wooding' which was a word used for collecting firewood. Oddly enough, every day a Mr Wooding used to walk up Ada's Lane from the next village to look at a small piece of ground he owned up nearby.

On the way across Mr Wooding would have passed the house of Mrs Whitton. She was rather a scary white haired old lady farmer who lived on her own, except for several dogs and some budgerigars. She owned one field and had a cowshed and a few cows. When going to school I used to leave my bike there as it was near the bus stop. Because she suffered from asthma she never cleaned the house for fear of stirring up the dust and setting off an asthma attack. So, inside the house the smell was terrible and occasionally she would invite me in for a chat. The dogs used to sit all over the chairs and one day I was just going to sit down and she yelled out "Daw'nt you sit in that one boy; it's got bugs in it".

Anyway, as Gooby got older she became ill and had to go to hospital where she had a proper bath for the first time in her life. Unfortunately, she died soon afterwards not from the bath, but from the effects of malnutrition. When they cleared out her shop they found thousands of pounds in cash hidden in tins all over the place. Although she lived the life of a pauper she had at one time received some education and had beautiful handwriting.

******

During those early post war years my father employed an ex-German prisoner of war (named Bruno) to help on the farm. He stayed on after the war and married a local village girl and remained in England until much later when his wife died of TB.

My mother employed a former evacuee to help in the house, who, for family reasons, could not return to London.

Bruno, late 1940's

Electricity did not come to East End until 1952 so the evenings were long and dark. Dad milked the cows not only by hand but by the light of a hurricane lamp. Indoors I did my homework by the light of an oil lamp and we went up to bed with candles like wee-willie-winkie. My mother cooked over an oil stove. In winter the bedrooms were bitterly cold.

Mum, Dad and Grandad c 1948 at Dollars Grove Farm

Of course we had no refrigerator to keep food chilled, and meat had to be kept fresh in a 'meat safe' which was a wooden box clad with perforated zinc. We did have a wireless to listen to, but this needed accumulators to power it, and we had to go to the garage every Sunday to exchange the flat accumulators for charged ones. On Sundays some of the villagers had permission to use the baker's oven in which to cook their Sunday joints and they could be seen scurrying up and down the High Street with trays of meat. The baker (Mr Eeles) made the most wonderful dough cakes, but due to rationing we had to save our coupons to buy currents and then take them down to him so that he could make the dough cake with our own currents.

The garage was owned by Ralph who was an extremely talented mechanic. Because no new cars were built during the war we all ran around in old pre-war models – ours was a Standard 16. These old cars needed a lot of maintenance as did the farm tractors and machinery. When my maternal Grandpa (Slippers) came from London to visit us he always used

Ralph's garage to repair his own car. He called Ralph a genius. In addition to the garage, Ralph also ran an old Bedford bus, and on Saturdays the bus provided a useful shopping service to Bedford on market day. He always returned promptly at 1 o'clock and on one famous occasion he even left his own wife behind because she was late. On another occasion the bus became stuck in reverse, so he reversed all the way back to North Crawley, a distance of several miles.

Ben Panter was an interesting character and he was the saddler and chimney sweep. In those early post- war years there were still a dwindling number of horses used on the farms and their harness needed running repairs. But most of his work came from repairing binder canvases, so every winter we took our canvases to be patched up. (These are the reinforced binder canvases that run between rollers and convey the crop to the knotter).

I don't remember much about going to the village school, probably because my mind was on the farm which seemed so much more interesting and important than school. I do remember my father telling me one day that I had to be quiet during morning break because he was attending an important funeral that day. The church and school are right next to each other in North Crawley, then as now. When I arrived home that afternoon he told me that all he could hear was me shouting in the playground.

The builder (Ted B) employed a small group of craftsmen who did running repairs to all the farm buildings and cottages on the estate, which was most of the village. When you needed a job done he always said he would come on Tuesday, but unfortunately – never which Tuesday. He had tools for all the windows and decorative carpentry used on the estate and could crop out and splice any damaged or rotten part. He was also a brilliant water diviner. When not doing building work he acted as Undertaker, and did the arrangements for my Grandfather's funeral when the time came. Ted Brandon's father was a very kind gentleman and a skilled carpenter. One day he arrived at the farm with a present for me – a brand new cricket bat made with his own hands

Harvest was always the most exciting time on the farm. All the corn was cut with a binder, stooked, then later carted and put into stack to await threshing during the winter months. The threshing was done by contractors who had their own tackle. Our contractor was a Mr Wooding who arrived each year with his steam traction engine, threshing machine and baler. Traction engines were good for stationery work, driving belts etc., but less so for towing. They easily became stuck in the mud due to a combination of their weight and steel wheels with limited grip. We often had to pull them out with our own tractor. Later the steam engines were replaced by Field Marshall tractors which were single cylinder tractors that we called 'poppy' tractors from the sound they made.

We also grew flax under contract and this was harvested by a 'flax puller' that they lent us. And then the crop was dealt with as normal, i.e. stacked and threshed. The important point being that the best linen fibres are contained in the root – hence pulling, not cutting. And of course the by-product is linseed.

A threshing gang taking a break at Dollars Grove -late 1940's. Large gangs were needed. The grain was taken off in Railway sacks that were extremely heavy.

Horse with nose-bag

We had an old Carter called Tom who used to look after the horses and get them in from the field early in the morning amid a great deal of shouting. He prepared their nose-bags with oats and chaff, and then he had his own breakfast in the barn, which was called 'Tom's Barn' for many years afterwards.

I also had my own pony called Polly - Violet that would throw me off at the least provocation

Me on Polly - Violet

Me cycling down the farm drive

At hay-making time I used to go horse-raking, and this was the first job that I did entirely on my own with a horse. As I grew older I used to drive the tractor for hay sweeping, whereby loose hay is swept up by the tractor and brought to the rick in a hay sweep mounted on the front of the tractor.

We had two Fordson tractors in addition to the horses. One day I went mowing with Bruno. I was sitting on his knee at the back of the mower when the seat broke and we both fell off backwards much to everyone's hilarity.

The haystacks were normally built in the same field where the hay was made, so in the winter we had to take the horse and cart to fetch hay for the cattle and sheep. It was cut out of the stack into trusses using a large hay knife.

At harvest time we used to cut the corn with a binder, as mentioned, and then stand the sheaves in rows of stooks or shocks. Many people from the village used to come to catch or shoot rabbits when news got out that we were cutting a certain field. Towards the end of the day the standing corn used to quiver with rabbits and eventually they wound bolt out and hide under the sheaves of corn, only to be caught by us throwing ourselves on top of them in the stubble. One evening we caught 47 rabbits.

My favourite job at harvest time was being up on the cart and loading the sheaves. There is a special way to do this and even as a young boy I became quite expert. I had my own fork with a short handle. When the load was complete I could lie on top and enjoy a short dreamy ride while wagon swayed and jolted to where the stack was being built.

We also made silage as seen here working with Grandad

Before we had electricity my father used to milk about 20 (pedigree) Shorthorn cows and he had a little three legged stool to sit upon, which actually only had two legs.

One day a cow with a new born calf severely tossed me in the yard, despite the fact I had been warned not to go near.

At that time my Grandad lived with us and used to help on the farm. He also did most of the gardening. Each morning he used to ask my mother what she needed from the garden and he usually kept us supplied with fruit and vegetables all year round. I used to help my Grandad quite a lot, especially with hedging, fencing and woodwork.

At harvest time my mother used to make tea and sandwiches for all the men in the fields and carry it to them in a large basket.

When I was about 10 years old my cousin Michael (who lost his father during the war) came to live with us so that we could go to Rushmoor School together. And being about the same age we had some great adventures, especially making rafts on the pond. We called ourselves names like Captain Redskull and Captain Billy Bones and we invented our own language called Wolonese. We also made explosive 'oggle' boxes out of treacle tins that used to explode on impact. After learning about Africa in geography, we burnt dry cow manure on our camp fires.

On summer evenings we used to play cricket in the meadow near the house and all the family joined in.

In those days I used to keep bantams and I had several sorts. I kept them in a small field called Bantam Farm, next to the garden. Fred, the game-keeper, used to borrow broody bantams to sit on pheasant eggs. According to him the best broodys were the feathery legged 'uns. Fred used to invite me to go beating on Saturdays and this was great fun, a way to earn money and a sort of repayment for the broodys.

Fred the game-keeper   *Bantam Farm - the unit that I built*

One of the most exciting things that happened was on a dark winter's night when my father was away at an NFU meeting. There was a knock at the door and a neighbour was standing there asking my mother to call the police. He had discovered some boys hiding in the wood who had escaped from Borstal.

Soon the village policeman arrived by bike and when he saw the situation he 'phoned the pub for volunteers to help round them up. Meanwhile he and my mother went into the wood and sat on the boys until help arrived. Michael and I kept guard in the field with our air-guns in case they should make a run for it. By and by lots of local people began arriving, including a police car. The boys were soon arrested and taken away. In the morning Michael and I discovered some things that they had stolen from the village, including a tea-pot, some butter and a pair of long pants. When the excitement was all over my father arrived home.

....

One day my sister, Judy, had tied some ribbons in my father's hair while he was having lunch. After lunch my father forgot all about the ribbons and there was a knock at the door. He answered the door and there was the GPO man who had come to mend the telephone. They had long talk and all the while the telephone man was giving my father very funny looks. It was only afterwards that my father remembered the ribbons

....

During term time Michael stayed with us at the farm when we both went to school in Bedford, as mentioned. During the holidays he went home to stay with his mother in Hampshire. Michael's father had been killed in the war (in Singapore) and so this arrangement made it easier for his mother to work as head teacher of the village school. In return, during the summer holidays Michael's mother and her partner used to invite me to stay with them in Mousehole where they had a fisherman's cottage.

The street in Mousehole where we stayed, and the harbour

During this time, we visited almost every beach in Cornwall with the chances greatly in favour of getting drowned. Fortunately, we were strong swimmers and never got into difficulties. Much as I enjoyed the holidays I was always itching to get back to the farm and help with the harvest.

Here is Michael (left) and me (right) at the beach.

Eventually all good things must come to an end and as Michael and I approached the age of 13 it would soon be time to go our own ways. Michael left Rushmoor School to go to Queen Mary's School, Basingstoke, where he later became head boy. From there he went to Southampton University where he gained a PhD. In due course I went to Bedford School, but Michael and I remained close friends all our lives.

At Rushmoor School that year there were two of us bound for Bedford School.

The other was a clever boy called David M. who lived in the Gold Coast. He was a very accomplished boy who was simply good at everything – Latin, Greek, maths, football, and he used to write his own plays even at the age of 12 or 13. In due course he got a scholarship to Bedford and later went up to Cambridge.

David M and I (middle back row)

One of the teachers was very kind to me and used to come out to the farm during the holidays to give me extra tuition in maths for the scholarship exams, entirely free of charge.

And so to Bedford...

Bedford was a huge school when compared with Rushmoor. I was there three years and I started in the 4th form, and then went up to the Remove, and finally the Lower Sixth.

Me aged about 14 getting ready for school

In the 4th form we were encouraged to keep a journal of essays, book reviews, articles or indeed anything that interested us. For example,

'Visit to a BOCM Farm.'

One day during the holidays my father and I set out to meet a coach-load of people visiting the commercial farm of the British Oil and Cake Mills Ltd.

We arrived at the farm which is near Epping Forest where we disembarked and were given lunch that consisted of pork pie, peas and potatoes, jelly, cheese and biscuits and beer.

The section of the farm which impressed me most was the pigs. First we went to the farrowing house which was beautifully heated with hot air and infra-red lamps for the piglets. They are kept here for about a week divided into eight pens each containing one litter.

Ten days later they are weaned and put into a Sowlac house. Sowlac is a specially synthesised food for small pigs. They are beautifully bedded in a long shed divided by partitions each with an infra-red lamp.

When they are thirteen weeks old they go into the fattening house where they are fattened up to twenty-four weeks old and then go out for bacon.

Next we were taken to the poultry section where we saw a thousand broilers and five hundred chickens in deep litter, and some young turkeys.

Last of all we saw the cattle. They were mostly Friesians and Aberdeen Angus. The calves were kept in little pens in a long shed. The stores were in a large covered yard, which kept them nice and clean.

We watched them milking about sixty cows, each with its own name and the amount of milk given during the last lactation painted on a little board above its head. There was also a huge bull in a pen on its own. With this and a vast sow I saw earlier I was quite taken aback as they took the biscuit for the largest animals I had ever seen – and I've seen a good many.

All too soon we were back in the bus heading for home.

(Author's note: In our household, BOCM always stood for – 'Beastly Old Cow Mixture')

'A Ghost Story'

It was the year 1850 and my friend and I set off for the north of Scotland to investigate the murder of a whole family living in an old Manor House.

The wind blew cold across the moor as we galloped towards the house, illuminated by the moon shining through the clouds and casting ever-moving shadows on the ground.

As we walked in the wind moaned in the cracks of the windows and doors, and the doors slammed and creaked. We ventured upstairs carrying an old lantern and examined the rooms which were cold and dark and almost empty except for an old bed here and there.

We had no longer settled down in our rooms next to each other, then I heard an uncanny thump, a door creaked and then slammed. Suddenly there was a deep growl.

In the room next door there was a mighty crash as if my friend had been thrown to the floor. Then slowly my door opened and a white figure passed through the room and out of the window. It was the ghost of my friend. He was dead.

Then my door swung open and the vast figure of and ape-like man appeared with face covered in blood, semi-toothless, and growling through his hairy face.

It was too much for me. I knew if I lay there any longer my nerve would crack. With a fantastic effort I leapt from the bed and beat him with a left and right to the face followed by a mighty blow to the heart. He fell with a crash shaking the whole house. In my rage I leapt forth and with my rifle I shot him six times through the heart.

I lit the lantern and walked into my friend's room where I saw him in a pool of blood, beaten to death on the floor.

This was the end of might have been a heroic story, but not for me with my best friend gone.

******

After the 4th form I skipped a year and went into the Remove where we were expected to do a serious amount of work in preparation for O levels. This was a very creative and hard-working period for me and I ended up with 9 'O' levels which propelled me into the Lower Engineering Sixth. By this time, I had more or less made my mind up to go sea and so it was to be my last year at Bedford. People wanting to go to sea in those days had to go at about 16 years old so there was no time for A levels. I didn't particularly distinguish myself at Bedford. I had some good friends, and we did a lot of sport. I was best at boxing and cricket, but only to 'house' level. I did score 55 runs 'not out' on one famous occasion. I was always aware that it was very expensive time for my parents.

Lower Sixth (me centre back row)

Meanwhile back at the farm much modernisation was taking place. Our first combine was a Minneapolis Moline. These were large, yellow, second hand machines imported from North America and were tractor drawn. Apart from the tractor driver it needed two people to operate the combine itself, one to raise and lower the header (cutting bar) by using a sort of ship's wheel mounted near the draw bar, and the other on the bagging platform. The grain was taken off in sacks and the sacks were shot down a slide onto the ground to be picked up later. In due course we moved over to bulk handling.

However, one summer holiday when I was 15 my friend Peter T (also from Bedford) and I went on an extensive cycle ride from Cranfield to Cornwall staying at Youth Hostels along the way. We took two weeks over it, sometimes stopping at the same place twice - if it seemed a good spot for relaxing. We were fairly fit to begin with because we all cycled a lot in those days. Some days we clocked up about 70 miles, and others much less.

Then in the Easter holidays of 1959 (my last year at Bedford) when I was 16, I went to the Outward Bound Sea School at Aberdovey. This was on the recommendation of P&O with who I was in touch about joining. (A number of Shipping Companies required potential Cadets to complete one of these courses before taking the plunge into life at sea).

The course was for one month and we had to keep a Personal Log Book. (for example):

Saturday 4th April

We were in the last carriage. The train came to rest in a tunnel. As there was no platform on either side we sat tight. Then in a few minutes the train moved off and passed a station with thousands of boys milling about – Penhelig Halt- we've missed the station! However, we got off at Aberdovey and soon a long, angry faced chap tore up in a Land Rover. After arriving at the OBSS centre we were allocated to Watches and settled in for the night.

Sunday 5th April

We got up at 6.30 am and had a cold shower and P.T. After breakfast we did some athletics which were quite good fun except I fell off a pole and grazed my arm. After that we learned about knots and splices.

Monday 6th April

Got up at 06.15 hours and after the morning routine we went to the wharf and set out rowing in a cutter – fairly hard work – and the afternoon outing resulted in most people having blistered hands and aching muscles.

Tuesday 7th April

Started off this morning with a cold shower at 6.30 am and cleaned out the hut. We then did some athletics, namely Putting the Shot (26 feet) and then marched to the wharf where we did some more knotting and fitted out the dinghy 'Curlew'. During the evening we had a hymn and a talk by Captain Fuller on Artificial Respiration. Won 'Best Watch Competition' today.

Wednesday 8th April

Got up at 6.15 am. Not very nice weather this morning but changing from cold and squally to fairly bright. After breakfast we went to the recreation room to learn about map reading, which was easy, as I had done it before. We then did some practice on following bearings e.g. 270 deg, 47 paces etc. Being Champion Watch for today our flag had to be hoisted, but following a practical 'joke' there was in inquest into who had done it after dinner. In the afternoon we went on a small expedition into the hills.

Thursday 9th April

When we woke up this morning it was raining and continued to do so for the rest of the day. After cleaning out the hut we went down to the river with Mr Smith (on secondment from the Commandos). We canoed up and down the river until about 11 a.m. when it poured with rain. After sheltering in a railway hut for a little while we canoed back on the ebb tide. In the afternoon we went sailing with Mr Pegler in a cutter. After which we went out on own and got back safely having gone aground a time or two. In the evening we had a lecture from the Merioneth Fire Brigade.

Friday 10th April

After getting up and doing the usual morning duties, we went to the wharf in the pouring rain and went rowing in a cutter on our own, and managed to do quite well against a strong tide. In the afternoon we went sailing in a cutter which was very nice as the weather had cleared...

Sunday 12th April

Today we were looking forward to a morning in which we could write our logs but it turned out that some of us were to do a canoeing demonstration to some industrial directors. We were transported to the wharf in the Land Rover and leisurely brought the canoes to Picnic Island beach in perfect weather. After some formation exercises we went in for lunch. In the evening we went to Church in Aberdovey.

Monday 13th April

After the usual morning duties, we went down to the wharf and went out sailing in No.4 cutter on our own. I got quite wet owing to a roughish sea. During the afternoon we went to the athletics ground and did 100 yards, 880, javelin, and high jump. So far a Merit for high jump, but 0.2 secs off 100 yards – hope to pick up. During the evening we had prayers and a hymn followed by a talk by Mr Allen on Malayan Outward Bound.

Tuesday 14th April

After morning duties, we assembled for our 1-day canoe expedition. We arrived back about a quarter to four and worn out. In the evening we had a lecture from our Bosun (Stan Hugill) on sea shanties and finished with the shanty 'Rio Grande'.

Canoe Expedition

At 8.30 this morning we went down to Picnic Island Beach equipped for our 1-day trip in canoes. We were accompanied by Mr Smith and Mr Lock – the Australian. We selected canoes and set off non-stop to a place near Dovey Junction, the first stage of the journey. We had a steady paddle and even got sun burnt. After a brief rest we set out again for a point as far again from Dovey Junction. This leg of the journey was much harder and I was glad to stop for dinner. After cutting the sandwiches and having our dinner we set off again for Dovey Junction – an easy paddle. We then came to the sea and had the wind against us making it very tough. Arrived back 3.45 pm. Distance 22.5 miles.

Thursday 16th April 'Golden Valley' Expedition

At 12 o'clock this morning we were briefed by Mr Pegler and then packed our kit bags. These were taken in the Land Rover to the wharf and we marched down at about 1.30 pm and found the Golden Valley not yet in. As soon as it came in we were on our way and over the bar, turned south and headed for Aberystwyth in a calm sea. The tide was low but we managed to dock and in the morning we swabbed the decks and sailed for St Tudwals Isles. After about an hour the sails were hoisted and we came into a rougher sea. By this time several people were already being seasick, and we saw some porpoises nearby. Eventually we sighted land and anchored, thankfully. That evening we had some supper and went on anchor watch. At about 6 am we were up again and immediately set off for Bardsay Island about 10 miles away. The intention was to pick up St. Vincent Watch who had spent the week there camping and bird watching. On finding them not ready we sailed round the island and waited. Eventually they arrived on-board in a dinghy which we towed back behind us.

Golden Valley

Four-day Expedition Monday 20ᵗʰ – Thursday 23ʳᵈ April 1959

We got up this morning at 5.30 and had breakfast cooked by Mike and Bill. At about 7 o'clock we set off up the hill at the back of the School with our packs that we had made up the night before. After going along 'Happy Valley' ridge the sun became a good deal hotter and we ended up carrying one member of the party's pack after the steep climb out of Pennal. However, we eventually sighted Dovey Forest and climbed down to the log cabin, 14 miles from the School, to have our sandwiches and make a cup of tea. Our feet were sore and our packs heavy. For the next 3 miles we navigated from a diagram through the forest and found a small magpie near the road. After going along the road we came to Corris where we stopped for an ice cream and then on to Aberllefenni where there is a slate quarry. After this there was only about 3 miles to go and we arrived at High Beech about 4.30 pm. We found the hut in a very picturesque setting of spruce trees equipped with Calor Gas for cooking.

The next day (Tuesday) we set out to do some forestry with one of the Forestry's Commissions men, Mr Carlow, with whom we did some felling and clearing of spruce trees in the forest. The axe work was quite hard as it was a very hot day, but in the afternoon Dick and I did some counting and stacking. That evening we had our supper of Irish stew and made bivouacs.

High Beech Hut

Today (Wednesday) we went for a 10-mile expedition into the mountains. It was a very nice day and the pace was steady enough to be enjoyed. On the way we saw Cader Idris and after dinner stopped at Hendre Dha for a brew of tea and explored the slate quarry. In the evening an increased number of people built bivouacs and I improved mine. Next morning, the day of return, we were woken at 4 o'clock, had breakfast and while the weaker, more blistered members of the party advanced to Corris, we cleared up and left about 6 o'clock. Outside Corris we climbed a steep hill and steadily walked along a ridge until we arrived at Tarrenhendre which we climbed and on whose slopes we had our sandwiches. After this the walking was much easier until we reached Happy Valley where we drank from a stream, having had nothing to drink for eight hours.

Cader Idris Expedition Monday 27th April

We got up at 4.45 am this morning, cleaned the hut, and set off for Penhelig Halt where we caught the train bound for Barmouth. Here we changed to a special train to Penlime Pool. Our party, being the slower, consisted of Rick, Dick, Martin, Charlie, Roy and I under the leadership of Steve who turned out better than expected.

We got off at the station and climbed steeply leaving Jellicoe watch to follow the wrong route. After about an hour and a half of 'not too sure' navigating we reached Cross Foxes Inn and the lake at the foot of Cader where the fox's path begins, this being the only route up the north face. We climbed steadily passing streams and shepherds' ancient stone huts until we came to a lake. The climbing was hard but we continued until we reached an even higher lake at the base of a 700-foot scree. We climbed slowly and methodically waiting now and then for Charlie who was already lagging badly, and here the mist began to form, making it impossible to see the summit.

However, at 11.30 we reached the summit and were greeted by Mr Walker and Mr Williams who were at the check point. After a brief rest we continued along the ridge in a bitterly cold swirling mist and soon found ourselves lost. But with the help of the cairns, a compass, and the foreboding giant precipice we found our track once again and descended to the second check point where Mr Smith and Mr Lock were waiting. From there we descended to Abergynolwyn where Mr Haylor was, and after a further 20 minutes walking we sat down and had our dinner on the side of a delightful valley with Cader still in the distance.

After dinner we advanced at a much improved pace. Eventually we arrived at Bird Rock, which needless to say we went round rather than over. Soon we arrived at Dolgoth with its narrow gauge railway and water-falls, where Mr Carlisle greeted us with some soup. Eventually we climbed out of the valley, which was an awful climb, being at least 45 degrees a good deal of the way. We then struck our old expeditionary route over the range containing Tarren Hendre and Taringasel. We continued along this path until we came within sight of Towyn and came to a cairn where Mr Davis was waiting. In another hour we were climbing out of Happy Valley and managed to keep smiling – or just about.

Off to Warsash

I left Bedford School at the end of the summer term 1959 and in September went to the School of Navigation, Warsash, which was part of Southampton University. This comprised a one-year pre-sea course for Deck Cadets, and counted as 9 months sea time towards the total of 4 years needed for Second Mates.

The School of Navigation, Warsash was founded by CAPTAIN WHALLEY WAKEFORD, O.B.E., F.I.N., Extra Master, in 1935. He believed that 'pre-sea training would be best undertaken in a specialised establishment that only trained boys for the Merchant Navy. This training should be very severe and strict and should weed out all those who were unsuitable either physically, mentally or spiritually').

On arriving at Bletchley Station I saw another Cadet standing there (Bruce P) in full uniform so we travelled together and became good friends.

At Warsash we learned Navigation, Nautical Astronomy, Chart-work, Seamanship, Ship Stability, Signalling, Knots and splices etc. in addition to the normal subjects of Maths and Physics etc.

We had ample opportunity to prove that we were of the right material, physically, mentally and spiritually! We were billeted in cabins of 6 people, two juniors, two intermediates and two seniors in each cabin; the routines were very strict and hierarchical. The whole School was split into Port and Starboard watches. At 6.30 am the bugle sounded for reveille and the juniors were expected to be out of their bunks and changed into running gear before the bugle call ended. Then they had to make their bunks by 06.35 am - at which time everyone went for a run up the road to a point determined by the duty Divisional Officer. On returning it was time for ablutions followed by tidying up the cabins and getting changed into rig of the day for breakfast. Most of the cleaning and tidying was done by the juniors under a good deal of threat from the others in the cabin. Then breakfast, then a brief session of signals from the morse lamp, then parade, then off to classes – except for those who were going sailing or some other activity.

Life was very hard for juniors. For example, at meal times the junior Cadets were made to sit upright at table and not permitted to allow their backs to touch the back of the chair, under pain of certain humiliations from the more senior Cadets. And they had other duties such as cleaning boots for the rest of the cabin polishing the deck etc. In fact, during the first term a junior's feet scarcely touched the ground from morning to night. Every week there were cabin inspections and the bunks had to be made perfectly, the floors waxed and gleaming, the clothes rolled up and stowed neatly in drawers and everyone in the cabin standing to attention beside their bunk. Imperfections were punished with 'overtime' which consisted of one or two hours work on the foreshore shovelling shingle and mud on our afternoon off.

Disciplinary matters were punished by 'drill' which consisted of running round the parade ground with a rifle under the supervision of the Master at Arms.

Cadets on parade at Warsash

Apart from looking smart we were expected to run everywhere, always with caps on. If a small group was going down to the boathouse for example, they had to form a small squad and go down at the double. Every evening the Duty Watch had to perform 'Sunset' which entailed lowering the flag in a little ceremony for which there was a 'Best Sunset Award'.

During the day we mostly wore a type of battle dress with boots and gaiters, but in the evening we changed for dinner into bow ties etc. and always toasted the Queen.

Warsash was well equipped with boats. We did a lot of rowing and sailing in 'gigs' and there was always was a (Cadet) Duty Boatman at the pier to take people out to the moorings. We had the sail training vessel – Halcyon, a Virtue, several gigs, a motor launch, a larger motorised vessel equipped with radar and other electronic gear used for instruction in navigation.

Halcyon - Sail Training Vessel

All Cadets went on extensive cruises on this vessel

Cadets sailing a Gig on the Hamble River

Halcyon was purchased to replace Moyana which sank in 1956. Because it happened only a few years before I went to Warsash, the event was well embedded in the psyche of the school. It is probably worth repeating the story of the Moyana from the Daily Telegraph:

HERBERT STEWART, won the first Tall Ships Race in 1956 as master of the ketch Moyana; but on the voyage home, he was forced to send out a Mayday call as the ship began to break up in a freak storm.
Stewart had skippered the Moyana since 1942, when the Southampton School of Navigation bought it to train "pre-sea" cadets.
Before the first Torbay to Lisbon handicap race for square-rigged tall ships in 1956, the school's director, Captain George Wakeford, told

Stewart that they should go in for it. Stewart was less enthusiastic - recording in his diary that he was not keen on ocean racing - but he duly set about preparing the Moyana.

The ship - 95ft long and weighing 103 tons - had been built in 1899. Because of its age, Stewart took the precaution of strengthening the hull, and fitting a new engine and sails. The choice of crew presented a problem. The five-week race would coincide with the run-up to the senior cadets' final exams, so Stewart decided to make do with 15 intermediate and junior cadets, aged between 15 and 17. Only one of these had ever been to sea before.

After recruiting his brother John, an experienced ocean racer, as a fellow officer, he trained his crew with three days' sailing in the Solent. During the race Moyana found better winds than most of its competitors and reached Lisbon in fourth place. Moyana was declared the overall winner after handicapping was taken into account. She also won the large class (over 100 tons), and the trophy for the fastest genuine training vessel. Stewart was presented with the trophies by the President of Portugal, before heading for home. Sailing north, however, the Moyana began to encounter ominously strong winds. Near the Scillies, a head wind sprang up from the east, blowing the ship off course. When the wind increased, Stewart ordered most of the sails to be furled.

At this point, his brother John went along the bowsprit to release the jib and was washed overboard. His lifeline passed under the keel, and it was a worryingly long time before he came to the surface. Stewart recorded in his diary his intense relief "when I managed to get hold of his wrist until others came to help". By this time, it was blowing a force eight gale and the Moyana was starting to leak badly. They were completely out of radio contact, and had insufficient fuel left to use their engine. Stewart decided to head for Cork in southern Ireland, but then, when the wind dropped, turned for Falmouth.

The next day the wind rose again, making a landfall impossible. They turned back out to sea as the wind rose to force 10, causing them to heave to, with the helmsman lashed fast. The leaks increased and the wind then rose to force 11, with gusts up to 80mph.

When there was just 30 minutes of fuel left for the generator, and the ship had started to break up, Stewart decided to put out a Mayday call. The *distress signal was answered by the Admiralty motor vessel Robert Dundas, which informed the coastguard at Land's End and Lloyd's of London. Eventually, the Moyana was sighted by an RAF Shackleton of Coastal Command, which used flares to direct two ships in the area towards it.*

While the Peruvian Reefer lay upwind, the steamer Clan Maclean came alongside with scrambling nets and pilots' ladders. The cadets leapt for the ladders and nets, and all reached the rescue ship's deck unharmed, followed by the petty officers and officers. The whole rescue took just seven minutes. The master of the Clan Maclean, Harry Cater, later recalled how Stewart had shown great concern for his boys and that all the cadets were in "great spirits".

The Moyana was taken in tow by the frigate Orwell, but sank when 60 miles due south of Plymouth, taking with it two of the trophies won in the Tall Ships Race (the main trophy had been brought home separately). Moyana's crew later all landed safely at Fowey, to loud cheers. Stewart was appointed MBE in 1957 for his achievement in the race, and his conduct during the rescue.

The year passed quickly and included some nice social events, dances etc. to which suitable local girls were invited.
Then I 'passed out' with Honours, having been 'Junior Cadet Captain of the Best Watch' and 'Vice- Captain of Cricket'.

Chapter 2

Going to sea

On 5th September 1960 I became indentured to the Peninsular & Oriental Steam Navigation Company and joined my first ship, the SS Sunda, in London Docks.

My father drove me down to London and on the way told me a bit about our relative John Ransom who was a Ship-owner and Shipbuilder in the 19th Century in Southampton. (An account of his life is contained in 'The Memoirs of the Hull Family'). I had with me my brand new sextant that my grandfather had bought for me.

When we arrived we found some of the other Cadets who were extremely friendly and helpful.

SS Sunda

The ship was loading general cargo for a range of Far Eastern ports. And on deck there was livestock, horses and pigs for Japan. Being a farmer's son I soon found myself on familiar territory although the shippers had put 2 Japanese grooms on board and 2 pig men to look after the pigs. The horses were housed in excellent stables, facing inboard and made from rough sawn timber. They looked rather like the old photos of the ponies on Terra Nova.

Once again we were encouraged to keep a Cadets Journal of everything that happened on the voyage. So here is an example....

Cargo discharged at Singapore

On arrival at the anchorage all dangerous cargo was discharged into lighters, of which 114 cases were for Singapore. The remaining cases were re-loaded on departure.

Whilst alongside, cases of brandy and cartons of milk were unloaded from the forward lock-up and the Bullion Room. From the Upper 'tween deck of no.1, 42 tons of sugar, 500 cases of tinned milk, various general cargo and machinery items. Some RAF trailers were discharged from the hatch-top. In No. 2 Upper 'tween deck there were rolls of newsprint, bags of kerosite, 770 bags of Ammonium Sulphate, and 5 cars.

..........my Journal goes on to include cigarettes, iron piping, wire netting, refrigerators, glass, personal effects for the RAF and chilled grapes that we loaded in Almeria.

....from hold 5, 500 bags of sugar were discharged for transhipment to Penang, and finally from the Boat Deck - 5 Pekinese dogs and 1 Alsatian.

In other words, a complete grocery store for every port.

There were six Cadets on this ship and we were divided into 3 on watch, and 3 on day-work, with the intention of switching for the homeward voyage. I was put on the 12-4 watch with the Second Mate. We Cadets had three double cabins between us and a study. And we had our own Goanese steward who waited on us at table, did our laundry and cleaned our cabins. This ship also carried 12 passengers so the food and living conditions were excellent. During the day the watch-keepers wore MN reefer uniform on the bridge and the day-workers wore boiler suits or dungarees. In the evening we all dressed for dinner.

Singapore 1960

The Cadet's Study was intended for Cadets to keep up with the correspondence course that we were expected do, which was supplied by The Merchant Navy Training Board. This served as a refresher to the knowledge that we had gained at Southampton; because on leaving Southampton we were mostly up to Second Mates level. The next three and a quarter years we would be concerned with practical learning on board ship. Because we had Indian crew, the study also served as a school room in which to learn Hindustani. (We all had a book called 'Malim Sahib's Hindustani'.

One of the abiding principles of the Merchant Navy, possibly the only one, was that Officers must never under any circumstance ask any crew member to do any task that he has not done himself. This is why Cadets spent a lot of time working alongside the crew, going aloft, greasing wires, chipping, painting, cleaning bilges, sweeping holds etc.

The round voyage to and from the Far East took about four and a half months. On the way back we loaded more general cargo, including resin, tinned salmon, timber, plywood, tobacco and frozen squid. On this homeward voyage I was on day-work.

Our journals were mostly intended to include things of a practical nature such as descriptions of – Fire Appliances, Emergency Fire Pump Operation, Hanging off Anchors, Noon Positions and Sights, Derricks and Rigging, Cargo Plans, Sounding Machines, Pipe Diagrams, Steering Gear, but we were also set essays by the Second or Third Mates whose job it was to torment us and mark our work.

First trip on SS Sunda

My second trip on SS Sunda quickly ended in disaster when we had a collision with another vessel in the English Channel at 4 o'clock in the morning, in thick fog. Our Engine Room was immediately flooded, all power lost, and we settled deeply in the water. The lifeboats on the starboard side were ripped off so we put all the passengers in the port side life boats together with non- essential crew and some dogs that we had on board. However, we took soundings all- round, and the ship seemed to stabilise. The Dover Lifeboat came out to stand by. Soon a tug arrived from Southampton and we were towed into dry-dock for repairs. So we Cadets had a few extra days unexpected leave and were then dispersed to other ships in the fleet. This collision made the second item on the BBC news that morning.

My next ship was the SS Ballarat. She was similar to Sunda but carried no passengers and was on the Australian run. She was a very fast ship with a service speed of 19 knots. She also had an 80-ton derrick. We loaded general cargo from UK and North Continent, and then back-loaded wool from Australia. She was the modern version of the old wool clippers. In addition to wool we carried a limited amount of canned fruit, peaches etc. We had a very good 'crowd' on this ship and I think it was one of my happiest ships. I did two consecutive voyages on this vessel.

SS Ballarat

My next ship was SS Garonne which was my one and only tanker. I did 6 months on her mostly trading from the Persian Gulf. It was quite a steep learning curve for me, but a very useful experience. I often sailed with a number of former Cadets from Warsash.

SS Garonne in heavy weather above, and in port

In her day the Garonne was considered a large vessel, but at that time tankers were getting larger and larger very quickly, the biggest being the Universe Apollo which we saw in The Red Sea and thought it absolutely massive at 80,000 tons.

On Garonne we had to make our own amusement because there was very little opportunity to go ashore at the remote oil jetties that we visited.

....

The next vessel was a passenger ship called Stratheden. I did three consecutive round voyages to Australia on this vessel, over the coming year. It was a very happy ship and a very happy time for me. I was the only Cadet on this ship and being quite senior by now I kept watch with the Second or Third mate. Normally P&O always had two certificated officers on the bridge of Passenger ships, one of whom usually had a Master's Certificate, and the other with a Mates or Second Mates Ticket. However, I was well enough thought of by the Company to be included in the 'junior officers' category, although uncertificated. I occupied a little cabin at the back of the bridge. This was a wonderful period in my life. We had a tremendous social life with the passengers many of whom were migrants on the outward voyage.

Stratheden in Colombo

Finally, the last ship of my apprenticeship was SS Iberia. We had five Cadets on this ship and were cruising out of Australia before returning to Tilbury. Again there was a wonderful social life for Cadets. We operated the launches when anchored off, kept watch, and worked with the Petty Officers - the Bosun and Yeoman of Mails.

Iberia: Gala Night

The Bosun and Yeoman of mails had many duties, and one of the least pleasurable was sewing any deceased person in canvas before burial at sea. The ship was stopped and the weighted body sown in canvas and lain on something like a door half over the rail, a short service was then held from the Book of Common Prayer (The burial of the dead at sea). And then a little tip, and the body would slide into the sea. The Bosun and the Yeoman of Mails were always given a bottle of brandy each for this job, which they drank – half before, and half afterwards.

My certificate for Crossing the Line in Iberia. I had of course crossed the line many times before but it was much more fun on a passenger ship

We arrived in Tilbury in a snow storm. Many of our passengers were Australian and had never seen snow before. I went back to Warsash to study for my Second Mates FG Examination and discovered that I had won the prize for the highest marks in the Merchant Navy Training Board Exams that year – a nice pair of binoculars.

....

By the time I passed my Second Mates Ticket I was living back on the farm. It was a very difficult farming year, and I stayed at home for an extended period to help with the harvest and the autumn ploughing. I was very much caught between farming and the sea, each one pulling me in different directions. However, I had lost my place in P&O so I applied to Blue Star and I did four voyages on the Paraguay Star to South America and back. Blue Star was owned by the Vestey family and most ships were intended to carry chilled meat from (Argentina among others). We also carried about 50 or 60 passengers. I was Fourth Mate on this ship and kept my own Bridge Watch.

S.S. PARAGUAY STAR.

Playing deck cricket on Paraguay Star

For a variety of reasons, I became unsettled at sea and took the decision to go home and help on the farm. Life at sea can be good but you have to sacrifice a lot of normal family life, girl-friends, life ashore etc.. Also it seems unreasonable that you should be swanning around the world while your parents and family are struggling at home.

Anyway, life ashore did allow me some time to take part in other activities and enjoy old and new friendships, to drive a car, to play cricket, and to pursue my interest in politics. I was mad keen on politics and quickly rose in the ranks to become Divisional Chairman of the Young Conservatives. I met many well- known people and we had tremendously keen organisation. I was urged to stand as a Parliamentary Candidate and even went to the elite Conservative College at Swinton for a course, but I was, I felt, too busy and too poor to attempt it -yet.

I had a very beautiful girl-friend called Christine who used to come with me to meetings and so forth, both in the constituency and also to Conservative Central Office in London. If in London we would go on to the Prospect of Whitby and afterwards driving back to Bletchley in my Mini.

Unfortunately, after a while we lost contact with each other for no particular reason. She went abroad, and we did not meet up again for another 50 years. To think if we had played our cards differently, she might have become the wife of an M.P.!

In the meantime, I met Maureen and it became apparent that the farm could not properly support two families, so I was faced with a dilemma. Should I return to sea or take another job? Well I decided to take another job and see how it played out. I took a job with a major Building Society in Northampton, and Maureen and I were married in 1969.

We bought a house in Nether Heyford and stayed there for just over a year when I was approached to take up a Branch Manager's job in Dorking with another Building Society, to which I readily agreed. We moved to a house close to the centre of town, near the office.

Here I had a relatively successful four years. I learned to play golf, I was Treasurer of Round Table, and I had a Company car, and had many friends in the business community. Our daughter Rebecca was born in 1972. We enjoyed several holidays abroad.

Rebecca

However, in 1975 my marriage to Maureen broke down and after much heart searching, I decided to return to sea.

Chapter 3

Extracts from letters to Cheryl 1976 – 1984

An explanation

In the summer of 1975 my marriage to Maureen broke up and I decided to quit my job ashore and return to sea. For me this was a very distressing and difficult time but I felt compelled to make a clean break from the past. I already had a Second Mate's ticket from my early days at sea so I phoned round several shipping companies and Bank Line offered me a job. I joined MV Meadowbank on 28.10.75 and did two consecutive round the world voyages. We left South Wales and went in ballast to the US Gulf and loaded general cargo for Australia, then up to New Guinea to load copra, tea, coffee, palm oil etc., for Europe. On the first voyage out of Swansea we dropped the pilot, the Captain handed over to me and went below and I was left nervously on the bridge peering into the darkness for the first time in ten years. Quite soon the look-out came creeping up to me and quietly said – Fire, Sahib! - And sure enough all the masts and rigging were covered in silvery, flickering St. Elmo's fire. I have never seen it before or since and often wondered if it was some kind of sign!

MV Meadowbank loading copra in Kieta, Bougainville

Loading cargo round the New Guinea Islands, New Britain, New Ireland and the Solomon Islands is a very interesting experience. Mostly we loaded copra, cocoa beans and coffee beans. The copra is brought into the main ports such as Rabaul and Lae on an assortment of local vessels from the outlying area in bags. Then the bags are loaded to the vessel and bled into the lower hold from the edge of the hatch-cover, and then carried in bulk. The 'tween decks are loaded with the bags of cocoa and coffee beans. This requires a fair bit of supervision. In places such as Kieta the nights are so dark it is hard to believe, and they are punctuated by frequent downpours. We had keep an eye on the radar at all times to try and spot the rain approaching from behind the hills in sufficient time to close up the hatches.

The labour are employed from local villages in rotation and mostly speak Pidgin English which is a creole language and the official language of New Guinea. They arrive at the ship decked out with birds' feathers in their hair. The signaller at each hatch, who tells the winch drivers when to slack away or heave, squats on the hatch coaming like a bird completely oblivious of the danger of falling into the depths below.

The business end of the trade is organised by one of the Directors, a much respected Captain Mac. One of our Indian seamen told me that when Captain Mac. was still sailing, and when the Indians needed to go back to sea, they would drift down to Calcutta Shipping Office from their home villages often many miles away to sign on. The Shipping office in Calcutta has a notice board with the names of all the ships requiring crew, and against each ship is the name of the Captain. 'And when the men see it is Captain Mac. who is there, all the men want to go! They think it is their father who is there'.

I much admired Capt. MacK and hoped that one day I could aspire to such a job as his!

In one of the small ports we met some Dutch Doctors and Nurses who were working at a small Mission Station and they invited a few of us to join them to witness an initiation ceremony that they had heard about in a remote village. So we went with them by the mission mini-bus quite a long way into the interior in almost total darkness. We passed several large snakes curled up along the road, and then we came to the village. In a clearing of the jungle there appeared the remains of a large fire with most of the villagers sitting round making a rhythmic sound by thumping large poles on the ground, thud-thud, and murmuring some chant. Then the boys appeared, naked except for penis gourds and head feathers. Each boy carried a large snake, holding it just behind the head and began to dance in and out of the embers, holding the snake aloft, and dragging its tail through the fire. This seemed to go on for ages and it looked as if both boys and snakes were a bit spaced out on something. Anyway, eventually we left and went back with a unique and indelible memory seared into our minds.

New Guinea is such an amazing place. To think that these villagers who are recruited to work as stevedores and so forth are only just a generation or so from the stone-age.

After eleven months and two circumnavigations we came back to Liverpool on 14.9.76 where I left the ship and went to Warsash to study for my First Mates ticket, and later met Cheryl.

First meeting with Cheryl to whom these letters are written

Warsash 2.12 1976

Dear bored young lady (26)

I don't know for sure whether I can assuage your boredom but I thought I'd like to be among the eight (ten, twelve ....) million people who are writing to you this morning as a result of your advertisement, (the like of which I've often thought of doing myself but never quite got round to it).

I dare not bore you with a blow by blow description of my few virtues and many shortcomings, but I will warn you that I am an ancient 34 years old and drive around in an equally ancient Minivan.

I'm also getting divorced, - which doesn't exactly add sparkle to a boring profile, - but all the same I should like to take you out if you are free one evening next week.

If you feel like taking me up on this free trial offer without obligation, I'm sure you would not be disappointed. Just let me know when and where to meet you.

'Till then I shall wait in trembling hope for the postman's daily visit.

Yours sincerely, Peter Hull

Warsash 29.1.1977

Darling Cheryl,

Saturdays without you are no fun at all – nor for that matter is any other day of the week when I don't know where you are and I can't even call you on the telephone. I suppose I really expected you to come home this weekend and I 'phoned and 'phoned to no avail. Serves me right I suppose for having such hopes, but it taught me a lesson in how much I miss you and how much I love you. I know it's easy to talk glibly about loving people but I've been really unhorsed by not knowing where you are and how you are, that I can't concentrate and I don't know what to do.

I read your letter over and over but it didn't really give me any clues as to how I should cope with such strong emotion. Perhaps the real shock for me is one of sudden re-entry into the human race – the stark reality that I need other people and you in particular. I suppose I've been orbiting just beyond the atmosphere and now I'm headed for some kind of landing. Will you be there at splash-down? Or will I land in the desert and be left to cry in anguish forever?

I miss you dreadfully, please love me a little, Peter

....

A little later I passed my First Mates Exam and in due course won the 'Cayzer Irvine Prize' awarded to the Southampton student obtaining the highest marks in the Department of Trade examination for First Mate (Foreign Going) in 1977.

....

Sunderland, May 1977 (Standing by M.V. Riverbank),

Staying at the Galt House Hotel, Sunderland.

Darling Cheryl,

....   just let you know all is well here and to remind you that I still love you. I shall be at this hotel until May 31st as we are now due to sail on the maiden voyage on June 1st or thereabouts. I have a cosy slanting room in the roof with three beds all to myself and miss you a lot.

Apart from that I met most of the other Bank Line crowd and they seem really nice. I spent the day at the shipyard and have been over the ship and I think you would be impressed to see it all. The shed is large enough to build two ships side by side, a real hive of activity ....

Galt House Hotel,

My darling Cheryl,

You write beautiful letters and to have had two of them already makes me feel very lucky.... hearing from you is a truly happy experience. I'm sorry you're feeling the strains of our parting – I do as well and can't really offer you much more philosophy on the subject than you offered me. I've come to regard it as going to work in large chunks and I hope that the coming test of absence doesn't prove too strong because I have high hopes of the future for you and I..........

....   MV Riverbank takes to the water at 2 p.m. next Monday and goes on trials about June 1st. The Company are making an event of this as it is the fiftieth ship to be built for them by Doxfords ....

All my love, Peter

Galt House Hotel, 20th May 1977

My darling Cheryl,

.... Next week ship 04 becomes MV Riverbank at the naming ceremony which is being conducted by a Mrs Philips. The 'float out' was a bit of a non-event really but I'm getting the photograph from the local paper so you'll have a record of the occasion. Floating out is not as dramatic as going down the slipway with a splash and the bursting of champagne bottles. Nevertheless, it's a bit of an event here on the Wear when a new ship appears and everyone stops work to have a look.

Spring seems to have come to Sunderland at long last and this week has been good for weather but bad for football, as unhappily Sunderland are going down to Division II next year. It's sad really because football means a lot to the people here and I like them very much. They seem to deserve a successful football team. Many of the craftsmen – shipwrights etc., at our yard deserve a good deal more than that. Oddly enough some of them are thinking of moving to the Isle of Wight where there are more jobs, and as I'm the only person around here who comes from south of Yorkshire they all assume I know all about the place and ask me.

On Saturday afternoon I visited Washington Old Hall – the ancestral home of George Washington which Jimmy Carter visited a short while ago. In fact, his cavalcade of cars passed over the bridge right next to the shipyard. Washington Old Hall is one of the few historic buildings I've seen up here because Washington is a New Town and rather bleak. However, I did go to Durham last week and found it very impressive....

Take care, all my love, Peter

Galt House Hotel, 24.5.77

Darling Cheryl,

In a strange way Galt House is becoming like home having been here for what seems like a year or two. We stayed in another place at the weekend which was a bit grim but close to the sea. So I was able to get out for some long walks along the beaches which are beautiful, sandy, expansive and very clean. Ironically some of the English National Opera Company is staying here this week - so I've had two introductions to them in as many months.

People don't seem to sing much these days, but at one time my Mother always sang as she did the housework. She taught me (in retrospect) that doing ordinary everyday things for people can be an act of love – and I think you are about the only person I know who knows what I mean. I was very moved by your poem – I wish I could write you one in return..........

Take care, with all love, Peter.

Sunderland, 29th May 1977

Darling Cheryl,

.... On Friday we went for a 'play around' in the North Sea on shipyard trials, which were a great success. There were 120 people on board all tripping over each other from 6 o'clock in the morning until late evening. We have to go through it all again next Tuesday on final handing over trials and then on Wednesday afternoon we sail for Hamburg. We are then bound for the West Indies and the Mosquito Coast....

Bilbao, 12th June 1977

My dearest Cheryl,

      I must say after leading a quiet life in Cranleigh all this exertion has come as a shock to the system – but no doubt I shall recover. In fact, I think I've lost some weight which is one welcome by- product. I've also got some of my work under control which is a great relief. Being a new ship there has been a lot to do in addition to all the normal things. Like sorting out and correcting a whole library of world charts for a start, and stocking up the dispensary.

      I loved your letter about the garden – you must be very proud to have such lovely flowers. I'm sure they are very lucky to have someone like you to tend them. I must say I miss the country and all the sights and smells that go with it. But when going up rivers and canals we do see odd bits of countryside.

      And being at sea is not so bad because the sea itself has a being all of its own.

      .... Much in love, Peter

Curacao, 24 June 1977

Dearest beloved Cheryl,

Yesterday was a wonderful day. I was inundated with letters from you when we called at Bridgetown. I was so pleased to hear from you and so excited to have your letters. ...The great thing about your letters is that they are not only readable but re-readable, and it's the re-reading of them that keeps me going.

I was wondering about your visit to the Surrey Show and was pleased that you were able to make it and had such a good time. I was also highly relieved to learn news of the tractor which has set my mind at rest!

.... (Seeing as you asked me for a blow by blow account of what I do with myself all day I'll try to give you one. It would be much better if you were here and could see for yourself because I fancy it will be difficult to imagine), however....

Wednesday 22 June at 09.00 hrs we are nearing Barbados. The Second Officer (me) is supposed to be the Navigating Officer and we don't know exactly where we are and the sky has been overcast for twenty-four hours, but at nine o'clock the sun comes out and I work out one half of a calculation that should reveal our noon position. At about 9.30 a.m. having sweated over the chart I go down to the surgery and give out aspirins and athlete's foot powder to ailing crew members. After that I go the bar which I also help to run and stock up the fridge and mop up ready for another day. Then I have three quick games of table tennis with the third engineer and beat him – to remain unbeaten so far this voyage. In fact, I can't find many takers now having beaten everyone who plays. At 10.30 am the steward brings coffee, after which I fiddle about until twelve when I go on watch again and with the able assistance of the Third Mate we scratch up a noon position by taking another sight. This puts us 37 miles from Barbados and within half an hour land is seen on the radar which vindicates my morning's efforts. We've already altered course about 20 degrees to home in on Bridgetown and the Third Mate goes down to tell the Captain all about it.

Now we have two sailors on the Bridge, and take the wheel out of automatic steering and go into hand steering as land approaches. We hoist flags and call up the Pilot on the VHF. He says 'Hello 'dere,' he says, you got to go anchor until 11 pm', so as we approach the anchorage the Captain comes to the bridge and second officer stands around like a spare part. The Chief Officer and Carpenter wend their way forward to the forecastle ready to let go the anchor. This is one of the carpenter's jobs but involves nothing to do with wood. The Second Officer plots the occasional position on the chart and switches on the echo sounder to see how deep the water is. The ship manoeuvers into position and drops the hook about one mile from the harbour entrance. At the critical moment the Captain's wife appears on the bridge and asks him - when for Pete's sake is he coming down for tea? For her troubles she gets stabbed by two eye beams.

At this moment the Radio Officer appears and tells me it is not 3 o'clock but 4 o'clock as he has just been listening to the local radio. The Second Officer wrings his hands on finding that they are on local summer time here and have not told anyone. So he sends the book around to let everyone know that the clocks which were retarded by one-hour yesterday are now being advanced one hour. This is the cause of some hilarity at my expense, but never mind I'll get them back at table tennis.

At last everyone has drifted off the bridge and I can work out my voyage abstract which concerns distances, speed etc. In fact, the actual distance was 3281 miles from Bilbao and only two miles different from my pre-worked distance of two weeks ago. The average speed was 18.33 knots – not bad for the first ocean passage.

At 4 pm I have a little sit-down and then drift to the bar for a beer before dinner at 5.30 pm. After dinner I then go around changing all the clocks back to what they showed yesterday, and at about 7 pm I go to bed. At about 11 pm I am roused again as the pilot has arrived and so I stagger to the stern with walkie-talkie in hand to join my band of about seven sailors and the Tindal (Bosun's Mate) to go alongside and tie up. Soon a tug comes and we make it fast; and then the vessel swings in the harbour and comes alongside. We make fast our stern lines and by about 1.30 a.m. all is finished. Letters arrive from home that are read voraciously, and at about 2.30 a.m. I am going to bed again. I get up again at 6.30 a.m. as the labour comes at seven to start work. I open the hatches and see the Serang (Bosun) about getting the cargo gear ready. It is very hot and humid even at this early hour. I hang around the deck until 3 p.m. and generally keep an eye on proceedings together with our Dutch Supercargo from KNSM who are the charterers. The cargo is mostly industrial products such as tractors, machinery, canned food and drink. At 9.00 o'clock I have a small troupe of sailors needing the doctor for whom I write out a form with their woes elaborated. They set off in the Agents car.

Meanwhile the money has arrived for those who are going 'up the road', so I dish this out. Hence the morning progresses between odd jobs until the doctor's lot return with their pills etc. Then I have a quick chicken curry for lunch and finish work at 3 p.m. Then I get changed and go into town and post a letter to a certain person, have a quick look round the town – lots of colour and happy faces, very picturesque. I can't stop long as we sail at 7 p.m. This involves going down aft with the same crew, making fast the tug, letting go the stern lines and we're off to Curacao. At eight o'clock I go to bed again until midnight when I get up for my watch until 4 a.m..............

M/V Riverbank

Nassau 8.7.77

Darling Cheryl,

......And as for you Cheryl Andrea – how I miss you. I'm sure it's thoughts of you that make me chafe so much. Yes, I do get your thought messages and I'm still transmitting – so don't despair – I love you and think of you all the time. I know there is a special bond between us which is quite unique – fused together as our paths crossed in the infinity of time. Jung believed in these special moments in time and I feel strongly that some unseen and friendly hand steered me towards you. I'm truly grateful to whoever it was because they've brought me whole new horizons of life with you. I think you are a super, clever, lovely, sexy person ....

All my love, Peter

New Orleans, 30 July 1977

Darling Cheryl,

I had a nice surprise yesterday – a letter from you that had been stuck in the system for a few weeks! It was one which you wrote to me from London and if I may say, as beautiful a letter as was ever read or written. Reading it made me feel very close to you.

Being in love with a girl who is a writer has the double benefit of everything one could wish for when we are together, and somewhat above average when we are not! In all respects I feel I am a very lucky person and there is no-one in the world who I would rather be with or receive letters from, than you.

Do you know, some days I think of you twenty-five hours a day, minute by minute, second by second and wonder if I is right that I should be so obsessed. Literally there are times when I can hear you talking, and the other day (as I was catching forty winks) your presence was almost tangible. I'm glad it's like that with thee and me. I'm very happy to be in love with you.

Did I tell you my brother stunned the entire world and got a First? Well he did, seemingly much to the amazement of all concerned, and I suspect – not least himself!

I love you so very much, Peter

M/V Riverbank, Napier, 13th September 1977

Darling Cheryl,

You must be wondering why I haven't answered your question about the OU. Well, the fact is I only just received letter no. 22 this morning and I'm sure anything I may say will reach you days too late, and your decisions will have been made already. If the decision has been made, then all decisions are for the best and must be stuck to. Either way, I'm quite sure the world will not end as a result. – Neither the world in general nor the particular world of Cheryl and Peter......

I'm absolutely sure that any plans we have for us can accommodate the OU for 12 hours a week. If you read the OU magazine, you'll find that people manage to do courses under the most weird of circumstances.

However, the whole subject of plans for the future does have wider implications from our points of view and it is something which I should be discussing with you now if you were here. Indeed, I have avoided trying to write on the subject for fear of making a terrible job of it. For me the whole question of the future has been shelved while I clear up the past. To some extent I now have achieved this and can tentatively look forward again and begin to make plans.

And you have every right to know to what extent you feature in these future events. Well, the longer I have been away the more I have come to love you. You play a starring role in all my dreams – waking and sleeping. All I want is to have you with me so I can love you and talk to you and try to make you happy: so that we can share life in all its aspects. There is nothing I wish for more than to have you as my wife and the mother of our children.

But that is a question I'm going to ask you in person when I get back, but perhaps you'd like to think about it in the meantime.

So my love, take care – I love you so very much.... Please speak to me in your dreams, Peter

Singapore, 3rd October 1977

Darling Cheryl,

.... I'm afraid Queensland had rather a quick visit from us as the sugar pours in in a matter of hours only, but takes a few days to get out again. You would have liked to prowl around Singapore today with all its bustle and fascination. I did a bit of shopping. I must say that is no substitute for the earthy autumn smells of the English countryside.

...... Whenever when I write to you I always get crazed and frazzled with interruptions and tonight is no exception. It's almost 2 a.m. and I'm in the ship's office doing the night cargo watch which is usually quiet – but tonight all and sundry keep sticking their heads round the door. Anyway, I have no news except that my new and special black Chinese ink from Shanghai just blocks up my pen something terrible, as you can see from the scratches and hear from the grammar....

I think of you always, all my love, Peter.

Bundaberg, 13th October 1977

Darling Cheryl,

.........At least the carriage of sugar is easy. It's just raw sugar like you buy in the health shop and they pour it in bulk, ton after ton, at a thousand tons an hour – and we are off, to be informed at the last moment to where or in which approximate direction to go. Usually up and down and inside the Great Barrier reef which is stunning. Then, into the Java Sea where we encounter numerous vessels under full sail: these are the famous Boogies of Indonesia.

I guess I'll be home in Bank Line's own good time. All love Peter

Boogie lying at anchor

Tokyo, 7th November 1977.

Darling, beloved Cheryl,

.... If you have an idle moment perhaps you would like to 'phone Andrew Weir (crew department) and enquire tenderly if they remember a ship called the Riverbank, and if so will the Officers be home for this Christmas or the next? You could then let me know and I could pass it on! It can't be dreadfully long now as six months have elapsed already since I closed the door on civilisation.

Do you realise, it's nearly a year since I first met you? That's another anniversary I wanted to celebrate with you. There are many things I want to say and share with you that I can't wait to get back now. I'm so looking forward to building a new life with you at its centre.

I love you, Peter

I eventually signed off the Riverbank in Singapore on 14.12.77 after a voyage of seven and a half months.

24 Bartletts Elm
Langport
Somerset TA10 9BS
tel: +44 (0) 1458 259292

03/10/2023

Dear Chris,

I'm so enjoying and impressed with your book (yes I bought a copy!) That I'm sending you one of mine that threw together after Cheryl died

Hope to see you soon

P.B.

Cheryl and I were married 23.2.1978 and went on honeymoon to the Greek Islands

Married Life

My next ship was MV Crestbank, another new ship built in
Sunderland. Cheryl joined me on the maiden voyage which
started in April 1978 and finished in November 1978. Cheryl
wrote some wonderful essays about this voyage which are
contained in her book 'A filigree of muted light'. Because we
spent such a long time in Indonesia I repeat one of her essays
here because it is not only beautifully written but describes a
unique account of a remote village called Malili in the Celebes.

Cheryl with me and some of the Officers off duty

MALILI / CELEBES - September 1978 - M/V Crestbank

We are anchored in a wide bay at the top of the two legs of Celebes and surrounded on three sides by dramatic mountain shapes. On the nearside the hills fall quite steeply into the bay, but on the other two, there is a wide flat land area – consisting mainly of mud and jungle, marshland and mangrove swamps – before rising into the mountains of increasing heights. Everywhere the vegetation is very thick, densely covering the mountains with tropical forest, and on the flats, coarse thickset palm vegetation interspersed by taller trees and creepers. We get a close look at this marshland on the way up-river to Malili itself. It is a native village about 7 miles from the ship, up the river – we go by lifeboat as the waters here are very shallow – even the lifeboat gets stuck in mud-banks occasionally! Wildlife must be almost entirely insects and reptiles, as birds and mammals would not appreciate the very dense forest and lack of light and space. However, we have seen a huge lizard on the riverbank, about 6 to 8 feet long, and I saw a very large green frog beside the lifeboat, swimming strongly.

Cheryl crossing the bridge at Malili

Malili appears quite suddenly after about two hours travelling past the jungle of the riverside. It is a quite extraordinary natural village. Rickety stilted huts of wood with thatched roofs, naked children in canoes racing the lifeboat, then giving up in an ecstatic leap into the river (Oxford and Cambridge boat-race could never be such fun!); very beautiful and gracious females, who even when old, keep their features strong and pure; and everyone, everywhere ready with "Hello Mister, Hello Boss" and innocuous laughter – genuine glee abounds without restrictions of the western or so-called advanced civilisations.

Children in dugout canoe

So even while we sit in this bay, waiting, we know how fortunate we are – to be in one of the very few unspoilt regions of the world left – and no doubt, in a matter of only a few years more, it will no longer exist in this pure state. Actually, about 40 miles beyond Malili, in the mountains, a small native village has been transformed into a 'new town' for the mine (nickel) workers. Graded dwelling areas A, B, C, D etc., according to the number of bedrooms and facilities offered, as well as the actual area of the town - administrators, workers, foremen – snobbery know no bounds! – but all the homes in each category absolutely identical bar the shrubs in the gardens, an airport, hospital and shopping precinct – this is to be the new residential style of Indonesia. I personally would choose Malili, inclusive of traditional facilities, be they primitive, every-time.

A FEW DAYS LATER

We have been on a very pleasant outing to a couple of beaches in the bay. They were only a few yards long but of fine silver sand – and with a wealth of shells and coral. As one approaches the shore, the sea is dark blue, then suddenly rocks and coral shapes appear and the water is transparent. One hangs over the side of the lifeboat dazzled by the clarity and the underwater world so forcefully displayed. The darting stripes of little yellow and black fish, the green and red parrot fish, the sleepy venomous coils of a sea snake, and the landscaping of clams and flowering seaweed, rocks and sponges, and shapes unknown and unnamed. And when we have landed on the beach, there are large shells – the spiny ones, the coiled and convoluted ones lying obviously on the white sand, but when one crouches down and runs an inquisitive hand across a cluster of pebbly particles – what colours and shapes are uncovered in miniscule shells and stones and broken corals – one is stunned by the enormity of love that has created such forms – and those ridiculous moments when one loses faith in this power – it is one's own blindness that is so gross.

It is so very hard to describe this part of the world – reading over these pages, I realise only too well how inadequate the words are, without the visual impact to compliment them the sheer width of this bay rising into the forested mountains, and the clouds that lie draped across the peaks or snuggle cosily into the upper valleys. The expanse of sky overhead, echoing the realms of silence and peace, the fishing craft that sidle past – homespun catamarans and small outriggers – with a friendly wave from the crew. There is poetry here – but it cannot be transcribed onto paper (certainly not by my unskilled hand) for it sings in its freedom, and it would be as cruel and useless as caging a bird to attempt to pin down such spiritual beauty in words.

Tomorrow we plan to explore an island at the mouth of the bay – shaped like a toggle, a long oval with an indentation across the centre where there appear to no trees, only low shrubs. It is approximately 6 miles away from our anchorage but should prove worth the deafening vibrations of the lifeboat as it has similar beaches, and therefore shells etc., as the other ones nearer us.

.... Well, we had a truly scintillating day. We moored first at a long stretch of sandy beach which had accumulated quantities of the larger shells, clams, cowries – and huge chunks of coral. Lovely yellow and black jerseyed angel fish abounded here quite fearlessly, and the water was a balmy welcoming bath to us all. The vegetation on the island is more varied than on the mainland, and gives the effect of a once-planned garden gown wild. Willowy and multi-branched trees grow along the shoreline providing welcome shade on the beach; palms of numerous varieties of course, but well-spaced and dispersed amongst the other plants. Many low growing shrubs and grasses cover the ground – and splintering the air is a continual cacophony of animal noises. At first we thought that the sound was made by a mechanical saw or it's like. However, we came to realise that the high pitched noise was in fact the crescendo of voices from crickets, frogs, birds, and many others: a very strange tropical mixture.

After exploring that beach, we motored round the island, eyes straining through the rippled surface of the water, to feast upon the strange world of corals below. We crossed over a huge floating shape and returned to be amazed by the silent and stealthy size of a manta ray, mottled and brown to blend with the shadows of its territory. Either it was stunned by the vibrations from the launch, or attracted by them, for it moved very slowly and without fear as we followed. And later we were shocked by the brilliant blue of a group of starfish – presumably such an artificial brightness acts as a deterrent for any predators – literally the colour of a bright blue rubber ball. But those corals - the shapes and hues – fans waving with the current, stag-horns proud and cruel, moss-like clusters clinging on rocks, pincushions of tiny stars and flowers, miniature trees branching out into those clear warm waters – all in tones of green, blue, pinks, rust, greys and brown. But when one looks through the surface of the water, continually moving and altering –through the aid of an underwater mask, the transformation is remarkable! Fish everywhere where before only those that crossed the surface were visible, and the coral itself becomes an entity on its own, whereas before it was a pattern, a dancing scene in the water. One is so overwhelmed that breathing is forgotten, and when remembered, a mouthful of salt water rushes in to choke one back into the realities of this solid world!

Before returning we chanced upon a small shingled beach for a last lingering exploration and there were the minute gems I had been searching for – those delicate works of art and sculpture in tiny shells; pure and blissful absorption! It was on this beach that I made my discovery! useless to describe it really (as you will one day see) but it appears to be a piece of coral, or on second thoughts an urchin, about one and a half inches by one inch, and chequered soft grey and cream. But drawn in the centre by a myriad of tiny pinpricks is a perfect star-like flower with five double petals. – It has already changes colour slightly by darkening – I only hope that it doesn't decay or decompose too drastically, as I am certain that apart from the joy it has given me in discovering such a treasure, that it is unique.

M/V Crestbank

After the voyage of the Crestbank I had accumulated enough leave to say at home for about five months until April 1979. In the meantime, I secured a Chief Officer's position with BM Ship Management in London. So my next ship was La Chacra which I joined in Setubal on 6th April 1979. Flat out La Chacra makes about 13 knots and stops for a breather now and then. She is an old gearless bulk carrier designed originally for the Great Lakes. Our first voyage was to Newport News to load coal. Cheryl did not come with me on this voyage because there was the possibility that she was expecting a baby, and in any case the last voyage on the Crestbank proved a bit too long.

Savona, 6th May 1979

My beloved Cheryl,

.... Last week was not a good week for us and I will explain why. As you know we loaded coal in Newport News and some more in Norfolk and all went well. It poured with rain but all my calculations worked out virtually to the inch, we got loaded and sailed on Thursday night. On Friday morning the weather was bad and I gave the crew some securing jobs and work round the accommodation out of the wet. Unknown to me in the afternoon three of them went forward to re-secure some drums when a great wave came over the deck and all but washed them into the sea. Two were injured and one just shocked and bruised. One had bad head injuries and we radioed the U.S. Coastguard now 200 miles away, and turned the ship around. Later (about 3 or 4 hours) they sent a helicopter out and winched the injured men off the heaving deck, but one died on the way to hospital. The other is now ok. As you can imagine it was a terrible day as what the crew do is my responsibility. I feel particularly bad about it. At least we were lucky not to be further from land as the helicopter was already on maximum range. The British Consul will be down to see us (me) about the accident sometime this week – to take statements etc. – so I shall be glad to get that over with......

.... I'm so excited that you are bulging visibly and I long for news. I'm so very proud of you my little earth mother and I love you completely.

All my love forever, Peter.

Savona, 12th May 1979

My beloved Cheryl,

     I received your letter and report about your visit to the hospital which sounded as if all was going well – I'm pleased to hear. I'm sure I'm every bit as excited as you are, and to be kicked by the baby at this early stage must have been quite a surprise. I wish I were there to share the excitement with you.

     Since we have been here the days have been almost perfect with blue skies, shimmering seas, really the first good weather of the voyage. Anchored next to us here, for we are still at anchor, is a ship called Andros Island – nice looking too, just to remind me of happy times with you on that Greek Island.... Had it not been for the accident I should say things were pretty good but of course I still feel a bit subdued about it as you may imagine....

..... My mind will no doubt turn to thoughts of Sundays in Aller which I miss dreadfully. This heathen life bears no comparison to the friendly village and the little church. It must be very nice to walk up the road to the church now that winter is over, towards Aller Court, and have regard to the goodness of the earth and the beauty of the spot. And so my beloved wife, thank you a thousand times for the beautiful letters which mean so much

     All my love, darling, Peter

La Chacra

Casablanca, 24th May 1979

My beloved Cheryl,

.... Well, my love the voyage is nearly half done now I'm pleased to say, and life on La Chacra is proceeding normally. We are at anchor off Casablanca waiting to load phosphate and the ship is rolling like a crazy horse. We are completely unprotected from the ocean swell and you'd never believe how we lurch and gyrate around. It is very exhausting to stand up and difficult to sleep. We should get to Rouen about May 30th and I have toyed with the idea of asking you to come over for a while, although your visit will be rather brief..........

All my love, Peter

Cheryl did come to Rouen and stayed with me on the ship

Le Havre, 14th June 1979

My beloved Cheryl,

     Almost the moment that you drove away in the taxi the loading machine broke down and so we were unable to complete. I must say I was glad really because I was able to get a night's sleep. It saved finishing cargo, doing a watch and being up all night. It's a shame that we didn't know sooner or you could have stayed an extra night, but never mind – we had a lovely time.......

Casablanca 23rd June

My beloved Cheryl

....   Well here I am again sitting down to write to you once more and trying to picture you pottering around the cabin as you were a few days ago. I did gather that the Leopard blacked out during your return crossing and I hope you weren't too alarmed - it's nice to know that other ships black out as well as ours.

     During the voyage orders came for us to proceed to the St Lawrence, but they have been changed and now we are returning to Rouen with phosphates again. I am sure you could come and visit again if you would like. Everyone on the ship is well and they enquire after you from time to time. The new steward with the ginger hair is getting the sack as he won't get up in the morning. Zoom-Zoom was sorry that you missed his Danish pastries which we had the other day.

I must say your visit to the ship did me a power of good. Not only was I overjoyed to see you but delighted to see you looking so well and happy. The first part of the voyage has been a bit trying at times but your visit seemed to mark a new chapter, as it were. I sometimes find it hard to believe how happy I am to be married to you.

Please take care of yourself, all my love, Peter

Dry Tortugas- 20th July 1979

Well here we are, 'here' being at anchor off the Florida coast waiting for a telegram to tell us where to go and what to load. Shades of the Crestbank, eh?

Having seen you off, we departed henceforth and had a good crossing. We got the holds clean in good time and I personally did very little thereafter. The reason being, that we have the luxury of two third mates and a second mate here, so I don't have to keep a watch. At present it is extremely hot and humid and the air-conditioning doesn't really work so it's a bit sticky and rains frequently. Today we had several showers of torrential rain. I have read several books and lots of your letters.......

All my love, Peter

Albany, New York, 29th July 1979

My beloved Cheryl,

.... Suddenly we have a telegram telling us to go to Albany to load scrap iron for Japan, so we are on the way. (Albany is about 100 miles inland from New York). As you know I volunteered to stay here a little longer and BM has promised to get me off in September. We should arrive in Japan during the first week of September, it takes 29 days from here to there.......

Your ever-loving husband, Peter.

Albany 1st August 1979

My beloved Cheryl,

The ship was expected to go to Duluth but there is a strike there and so we have wound up in this funny place loading two million dollars' worth of scrap. The scrap is pouring in nicely and the hatches look just like Bill Tucker's scrap yard – full to the brim with old ploughs, axles, engines, wheels etc., just crashing in.

Last night the Captain, Chief Engineer and I went out to dinner and had Maryland crab and Idaho trout, all washed down with a few screwdrivers. Yesterday the local newspaper reporter came on-board to do a feature about the ship and take photos. They interviewed several people and had a look round and a chat with me and asked whether I missed you and that sort of thing. Of course I told them I did. I also got a haircut the same afternoon and bought a pair of jeans in a sale. As if that's not enough social life, we are having a cocktail party on board in New York for the Charters, Agents, and Shippers etc.

By the way, I am flying home from Los Angeles about August 27th.

All my love, always, Peter.

I was home on leave until 3rd November 1979 when I was recalled to M/V La Cordillera, one of the new GB vessels that were under BM Management. These ships were quite advanced for the day being open hatch with travelling gantry cranes. Unfortunately, this ship had been in a collision in the Bosporus and was in dry-dock in Greece undergoing repairs. So here began my relationship with GB that was to last another 20 years.

La Cordillera

This was rather awkward for us and for me because Cheryl was expecting to give birth during November and I had hoped to be at home until then.

Elefsis, 3rd November 1979

My beloved Cheryl,

.... 'Many Happy Returns of the day', my love. How I wish I were there to celebrate with you.

.... On the train from Taunton I accidently sat next to the Deputy Head of Plymouth College of Nautical Studies. He was going to London for a meeting and told me of some courses which they run for people with Masters 'tickets, such as management course etc., which sounded interesting.

       Ever yours, Peter

Elefsis, 8th November

.... Two days ago we had a little party with some of the people from a Russian ship at the next berth. Some (2) of their stewardesses came, so with the wives from La Cordillera, there was dancing and drinking. I of course behave honourably! Two Commissar types came to keep an eye on things and they dressed in red shirts, red ties and socks, with blue suits – while the others were in casuals, and at 10.30 p.m. prompt they all rose as one and left. But during the proceedings the two Commissars went out for a natter and came back to me (only me) and said, "We very much like for you to come and live in USSR". So you see I had an invitation to defect but decided to stick with Somerset.

       Everyone thinks BM were rotten to send me away on the brink of fatherhood, and so do I, but I suspect they are short of Chief Officers at the moment. Tonight we have been hold cleaning again – so back to the old routine.

I pray everything will be alright, I love you, Peter

Barcelona 19th, November 1979

My beloved Cheryl,

..... In Sagunto the Surveyor took me out for a brief lunch-time beer at a bar on the seafront and we had olives stuffed with shellfish and roasted almonds. The Agent came too and in addition I was given some wine from the cement factory.

The ship is being fitted with a Satellite Navigator so it will have just about everything except ink! I shall be glad when loading is finished as I'm always afraid it will go wrong just towards the end. The limiting factor is the draught in the Suez Canal. The Chief Steward – La Chacra Chief Steward's uncle – has some Champagne in store ready for a celebration when your news comes of the birth.

I do hope everything is going well my love. I am constantly thinking of you and the unborn baby, all my love, Peter

Jeddah, 1st December 1979

My beloved Cheryl,

You can hardly know what a happy and proud husband and father you have made me become. You are a beautiful and lovely wife and I love you too much. Hardly a moment passes without me thinking how lucky I am to have you, never mind a son as well.

I must say the news came as a great relief after all the weeks of waiting and I had to make 'Liz say it twice before I completely believed her. Mind you the reception on the 'phone was dreadful. Everyone on the ship was delighted as they had become almost as anxious as me.

I continue to hope and pray that all is well with you both and I am sure that everyone at home is overjoyed. The crew (Somalis) are very pleased, as having a son is very important to them.

I love you, Peter

James was born on 27th November 1979

Marmagao, 9th December 1979

About an hour before we left Jeddah your letter arrived (date 28 Nov) giving me all the details of the great event. How happy I was to hear from you and to know that all is well with you and James.

Life has been a bit hectic just lately. The spell in

Jeddah was very busy, working round the clock and we finished in about three days and then received orders to go to India. We are due to arrive in Japan just before the New Year so we shall have Christmas somewhere in the China Sea. The cake has already been made and I expect everyone will make the best of it.

Your loving husband, Peter

At Sea, 24th December 1979

Well, here we are on Christmas Eve wallowing about on the edge of tropical storm 'Ben'. Despite which, and the violent rolling, I am thinking of you as always. I guessed it would be just our luck to have a storm at Christmas, and here it is.

And, my love, I had your telegram yesterday courtesy of BM, which was a great surprise and a prized piece of Christmas news in this lonely and far off spot. Thank you for sending those loving words my beauty, they brought me great joy and pleasure.

We didn't stop long in Goa, just twenty-four hours for a full load of Iron Ore – and off again, so I can't tell you much about it. However, we are bound for Sakai, near Osaka, and then British Colombia to load timber and wood-pulp for Portbury. So we expect to be there (Portbury) about the end of February. I hope you will be able to come and meet us. I fear young James will be grown up and smoking a pipe by the time I see him.

.........Your loving husband, Peter.

Watson Island, Prince Rupert, 14th January 1980.

My beloved Cheryl,

It's over a month since the date of your last letter so I've had no news of you since December 10th. As you know we paid a brief visit to Japan and left in less than 24 hours. Since then we have been battling gales and storms all the way across the North Pacific. We are now at anchor off Prince Rupert waiting for daylight. We struggled to clean the holds for about ten days with the ship rolling up to forty degrees either way and us diving into blocked bilges – very cold – and since then snow almost every day.

I suppose little James is not so little any more. It seems years since 'Liz phoned the ship with the news, but it's only six or seven weeks ago. I hope the little mite is coping with the cold, fatherlessness, about-to-be-blown up- in-a-nuclear-war, in a hostile no-money world. You should tell him things can only get better.

Your loving husband, Peter.

Harmac, 19.1.1980

My beloved Cheryl,

.... The place we have just left was called Watson Island, near Prince Rupert and not far from Alaska. It is a small place – just a jetty next to the pulp mill and a canning factory, a few houses and a shop. It's not too cold though, just about freezing with occasional snow showers and everywhere is very picturesque. All around are mountains covered in spruce trees, and bays, sounds, waterfalls, and mile on mile of completely unspoilt land. We are now going all the way to Vancouver by an inside passage between the islands which is very smooth and scenic. We have to load more pulp and timber. We have a GB Supercargo here so life is fairly simple for me. I have your photo here framed beside me to keep an eye on me. The Supercargo says you look like the lady who should have launched the ship, what with the hat and the flowers etc.

We are still expecting to arrive at Portbury about the end of February.

Take care, love as always, Peter

And so I signed off in Portbury on 26 February 1980. Cheryl met the ship on the dock with James who was exactly three months old when I saw him for the first time. We all went home for some well- earned leave until 22.4.1980 when I joined La Primavera, an almost identical ship to La Cordillera. To a large extent the correspondence continues in the same vein with certain exceptions..........

La Primavera

Munguba 26.6.80

My beloved Cheryl,

.... After writing to you about the accident, we then had
the GB party which was almost as bad in its own way. About
twenty-five people arrived, the Charterers, the Bank of Brazil,
the Fertilizer Company, etc. and to my horror nothing was
ready! (Not my department the food and drink). Anyway we
found some whisky and settled them all down in in the
Captain's room and I struggled to inject some hospitality into
the air. I worked very hard to make the thing seem organised
and soon we went down for the Buffet. I was the only one who
could open wine bottles, the beer was warm, and I rushed
around helping people to their food. 'Where are the stewards
hissed the GB representative to me. 'Gone ashore' I hissed
back. Mercifully it seemed better at the end than at the
beginning, but only after copious Drambuie's and lots of my
charm. I showed then round the ship and eventually they all
trooped off calling me 'Captain' – very embarrassing. Heaven
knows what GB thought of it all, I thought it was dreadful, and
feel exhausted just thinking about it.

But that was only the beginning, we then heard that the next cargo is to be Kaolin – yes the stomach powder (China Clay), and that the holds have to be spotless and freshly painted. (At least one hatch for this cargo – the other cargo is pulp). So in Santos we have some long sessions of cleaning and painting, and today we have sprayed over an acre of paintwork. It is very difficult to fit this work in during discharge, what with sulphur dust blowing everywhere, and the cranes not always being available. One has to do down standing on the grab with the spray gun as the holds are forty-five feet deep, and one of the youngest crew did nearly all of it himself. It is like circus without the safety net. One day we worked at it from 5 o'clock in the morning until 10 o'clock at night. I went to bed at midnight, but at 2 a.m. the wires on the crane pulled out so we had to turn to and fix that. And it took the rest of the night: and so began another day somewhat similar.

In Santos there is also 'Hellfire Corner' to divert the attentions of the lusty sailor. Here are the girlie bars where everyone's dream can come true for twenty dollars. The owners of the jetty where we are berthed even lay on a bus back from town at 6 a.m. Some went ashore with a couple of hundred pounds and didn't come back until it was all gone!

.... Still the saga of the hold painting continues and today I sprayed one myself. On these ships it is strictly verboten to open the hatch at sea or un-park the cranes, but we did this regardless. These days there are great pressures to have everything ready without loss of time and so we slowed the ship and flogged the log to read 'heavy rain' and I swayed around in a little basket squirting silver paint. 'You look like the tin man', said one of the crew as I emerged all silver some three hours later. It took ages to get all the paint off me and still there is some on my eye-lids making me look like Danny-la Rue after a party, with red eyes and silver surrounds. But the worst thing is my knees. Because of the swaying around I kneel in the basket for safety and after all morning I could hardly walk. Obviously there are special muscles in the leg which I do not have. No doubt they would be better developed if I prayed more, so I suppose it is judgement on me. I well remember the Retreats at School (which I didn't attend), where boys frequently fainted from all the time and pain spent kneeling. I fully appreciate the misery they must have endured.

Anyway the job is done. I always wanted to go up the Amazon, but now we are here I'm not so keen. Everything has to be locked up on account of thieves and pirates, and what with the general confusion over loading, the ultra- clean holds, and tricky navigation through the shoals, I think ship-owners get their labour cheaply. I also expect an invasion of Jungle-bunnies for the delectation of the crew, and no doubt that may cause problems as well. (I don't know what Amazon jungle-bunnies are like but the New Zealand ones are quite nice. They just invite themselves on-board for the duration. No-one usually minds as long as there is no trouble, you just have to broad minded and let the crew do their own thing.

The river here is like tomato soup – hot, red and thick looking. It is very wide where we are at the moment, but the Jari River is only quite small. ....

Munguba, 2nd July 1980

My beloved Cheryl,

    I was afraid this place would be a problem and how right I was. After all our efforts to clean and paint the holds, two of them failed. They looked really smart and the crew were browned off to say the least. The first trouble was that a sudden rain shower came and wetted the kaolin hold which we had to mop out, and a wretched Japanese chap took photos of us all – tired and dirty – mopping the hatch and cleaning up. They even complained about tiny specs of dirt that when collected together would not fill a match box. It finally stopped raining and the hatch passed. Meanwhile (we) had to scrape the bottom of the other hold which had been made rusty by the previous sulphur cargo. Anywhere else it would have been perfect for pulp – but not here. It was Sunday night and the crew had had enough and they all went ashore to the little bars and shacks across the river. (Just like Malili with lots of friendly girls and cheap beer). Muggins here had to scrape the hatch himself and we finally painted it next morning. It was very hot, tiring and depressing work especially after risking our jobs/lives trying to paint the holds at sea previously. That night I could have cheerfully walked off and nearly did. It had already been a long day and night, but the next day was even worse.

The kaolin loading went slowly and towards midnight I checked the draught for a tonnage check. My figures disagreed with the shore balance by over 800 tonnes. I checked and re-checked and decided that we had all we needed. No-one believed me as the shore balance was new. I tried to phone the boss of the place, but no-one spoke English and no-one in authority was there or available. So in the light of day, after two hours sleep, all sorts of sparks began to fly, allegations, statements to make etc. Unfortunately, there are no surveyors here to back one up regarding quantity.

After two days of extreme pressure and harassment we arrived at the pulp berth and the Port Captain invited me to "The Club" where we had a bit of a party. I was glad to get off the ship I can tell you. It was quite a lively affair – I think all the oxygen in the air gives the Brazilians their zest. It was a typical ex-pat type of place with Portuguese, German, French, and Canadians etc. all together. The Jari Project is quite startling in scale and there is a full account of it in the National Geographic, May 1980.

All my love, always, Peter

****

I thankfully signed off La Primavera in Kittimat on 4th August 1980.

My next ship was M/V La Costa – a sister ship of La Cordillera which was mostly employed on 'the cement run'. This was mainly from Spain to Jeddah repeatedly, with some other ports thrown in. Life on the ship continued normally with occasional moments of interest. I joined La Costa on 6th October 1980 in Montreal.

******

Yenbu, 7th November 1980

My beloved Cheryl,

……… The new Captain is helping me by showing me all the paperwork entailed in his job, and generally getting me knocked into shape.

I visited the local town one evening and it is just like Basrah, some nice old buildings, some nice new buildings and a lot of rubbish in between. The streets are a mess really with paper, cardboard and dumped cars etc. There is a market and all the shops sell duty free cassettes, radios, watches etc. I only saw a few veiled women scuttle past, otherwise all men. No booze of course but I had an orange drink and a kebab. We had a fair bit of trouble getting in and out of the gate where the Saudi guards make up the rules to suit themselves. The crew get along alright as they speak Arabic and today being Friday I gave them a half day off to visit the Mosque – the wailing from which you can hear from the ship.

However, the cement plant is run by GB and the Norwegians are friendly and live in a little compound about five miles from the town. I went one afternoon for a swim in their pool and in the evening for a little barbecue with the Captain and some others from the ship. It was very nice but 'dry' of course. We had some Saudi wine which is alcohol free and tastes like jam.

Before you get there, the road peters out (funny word that) and there is a bit of desert to cross and you have to avoid boulders, burned out exhausts, old wheels etc. at high speed. One Arab family lives on the compound but of course the wife cannot swim or socialise, but the children run around. They have a thin cat with three kittens.

There is a lot of work to do on the ship and we are busily engaged in painting the cranes and scraping off layers of old cement before South Africa. We are going to Russia first, but the prospects are for Durban. When the new Captain joined he had letter from the office saying I would definitely go home from Durban about a week before Christmas.

All my love, Peter.

La Costa, Novorossiysk, 15th November 1980

.... My geography is improving somewhat as this part of the world is completely new to me. We came up past the Greek Islands, through the Dardanelles, the Bosporus and the Black Sea. We anchored in fog at Istanbul which seems to be an amazing place, and great Mosques etc. were revealed when the mist cleared. It is quite a busy passage up here and not at all like the long drags half across the globe to which I have become used. There is lots to see and some of it very interesting. I have not yet sampled the delights of Novorossiysk, but may do one evening soon. The town looks pretty grey, but maybe that is something to do with the Cement works which cover the whole place in a pall of smoke. There is a huge hill just behind here which is being dug into and turned into cement, I presume. Fortunately, everything is at a slow rate and we shall be here for at least a week. It is all very bureaucratic and I need a pass to go down the gangway to look at the ship. A little soldier stands there and freezes for twelve hours a day.

Touch wood life on the ship goes on smoothly and I must admit to being well occupied, and more relaxed than I have been for a long time. You would like the Captain and his wife who are very friendly and well adjusted. I cannot speak too highly of them. Perhaps you will meet them sometime. He has been giving me a lot of help with his side of the job and let me bring the ship into this port when we arrived. So I'm getting some practice at ship-handling etc.

.........well, last night I sampled the delights of Novorossiysk. A bus comes and takes people to the Seaman's club which is about the only place to visit except for a bar called the Brigantine which I have not yet found! Although the general atmosphere of the town is rather dull and run down the club was quite lively. They had a dance with live music and wine at the bar. I drank too much and fell backwards onto the stage much to everyone's delight. At eleven thirty the whole thing wraps up and you have to be back by midnight on pain of the salt mines. The Russian wine is not too bad but today I had a mighty headache which I suppose serves me right.

My birthday has been moved to the 20th on account of three others having birthdays quite close. As a result, Mrs Captain has decreed that a joint party is to be held. It should be a bit of an occasion, but we are very low on drink, except martini. No doubt we shall muddle through. We are trying to get something here, but even fresh water is a problem. We finally got permission to paint the ship's side after a struggle with the immigration.

Today I have been showing off my welding prowess, as I have been making some parts for a boat which we have. The Chief Engineer said he had seen Engineers do worse so I was quite flattered. The Chief is the Dutchman you met on La Cordillera.... I miss you Daisy May, Much love Peter

Port Said, 27th November 1980.

My beloved Cheryl,

     My own birthday party went with a swing and the wives made some punch and the boys got some girls down to the ship and there was dancing and a super buffet, with birthday cake and all sorts of things. The Russians left about 11 o'clock so the party fizzled out and everyone got a night's sleep.

     Every cabin and person on the ship is inspected on arrival and departure and the ship is guarded round the clock. And out by the Port entrance great searchlights sweep the water to ensure no small boats dash out for a rendezvous. I think life in Russia must be like life in wartime Germany. Such officialdom.

     Saudi is not much better. You remember that nice bosun –Trevor – on La Cordillerra, well, a few months ago his little twelve-year-old daughter phoned the ship in Jizan to say his wife had tried to commit suicide and all the power and influence of GB could not get him home. They simply would not stamp his visa to allow him to leave and he had to wait until Barcelona. The Norwegians even offered £500 of their own money just to get a stamp on a piece of paper. Such is the humanity of the Saudi Arabians.

     All my love, Peter

Jizan, 5th December 1980.

My beloved Cheryl,

Jizan is a bit off the beaten track but the cement plant is the same as at Jeddah. i.e. A converted tanker with a bagging plant on board. We discharge in bulk and lorries drive away with bags. Another one is being built for Sudan and another ship in Jeddah for animal feed. All livestock has to be imported live into Saudi, so at the time of the Haj there are huge pens of sheep all being fed on GB rations whilst they await the Muslim knife. Almost next to the cement berth, arrive little livestock ships with sheep and camels from across the Red Sea. The sheep are brownish with floppy ears and they get thrown out of the dhows any old how, while the camels are slung with a belly band and hoiked out on derricks.

Anyway Jizan is another Umm Qasr sort of place and hard to get to. We have to use a home-made chart for the last hundred miles through the reef. It was drawn up by Hansa Line (remember them?) for their ships which sometimes came here. It's quite a nasty passage through the reefs but on the way we stopped for some adventure (because you cannot transit by night). On his last voyage the Captain had seen the wreck of a Greek ship and wanted to visit it, so we put the boat down and motored over to it about 3 miles away. Or rather I did, together with a little band of pirates all armed with tools, crow bars and grappling hooks to scale the side and rip out souvenirs. The wreck is on a reef about a hundred miles off the coast. So we arrived and boarded to find the thing completely pillaged, but we did manage to salvage some brass port holes and two superb ship's wheels each one about five or six feet in diameter. We had to saw through 3-inch steel shafts to get them off.

I think I shall squeeze home from Durban just in time for Christmas, probably the 22nd or 23rd.

All my love Peter

French Cadet Pierre sawing away

I signed off La Costa on the 21st December 1980, and went home for Christmas. After which I went down to Warsash to study for my Class 1 Masters FG. I remained ashore for nine months - studying and on leave until 14.9.81 when I joined La Estancia, a similar GB vessel on the same cement run. I was on La Estancia for just over a month before getting my first command.

During this time, we moved house and bought The Woods at Charlton Mackrell, a 700-year-old, Grade II listed cottage standing in about three quarters of an acre of garden

The Woods

La Estancia – covered in cement

La Estancia, Port Said, 6ᵗʰ October 1981.

My beloved Cheryl,

Life on La Estancia has been fairly busy on this run with only a few days between ports. We managed to scrape the bottom on the reef going into Jizan but didn't get stuck and have no apparent leaks. So having visited a wreck here last year, we nearly became one this year....

All my love, Peter

La Estancia, Alcanar 15.10.1981

.... I must say life on this ship has been rather a bleak experience to date, what with the run to Saudi and the lack of news about whether I shall be back in December in time for the birth. However, I do have some moderately good news as one of the people came down from the London office and we discussed your forthcoming confinement. He said they will do their best to get me home irrespective of distance.

However the weather here is beautiful at present and Alcanar is a small place not far from Valencia. The cement works is perched at the bottom of a hill into which they dig for whatever it is they make cement out of. There is a little beach nearby and a small town called San Carlos de la Rapide.

....   All my love, Peter

La Estancia, Alcanar, 20.10.1981

My beloved Cheryl,

...... yesterday we had some rain which is just about the worst thing when the ship is covered by a snow fall of cement. I paid a brief visit to the local town, but the shops were shut, so I had to get someone to buy the post-cards I am sending to James and Rebecca.

As we have different sorts of cement the loading is a trifle complex and the surveyor comes down most days for a check. Everyone is sick of cement which we have to sweep off every day. It takes all five Cadets the whole day and then the next day they start all over again.

Not much to write about, all my love, Peter.

I signed off this vessel in Suez on 29.10 81 to take up my first command as Captain of La Cordillera which I joined in Portbury on 21.11.1981. This was a proud moment for me. Cheryl and James came down to the ship with my Mother and Father. All the effort and sacrifice of the last 5 years suddenly seemed worthwhile.

La Cordillera, Rouen, 30th November 1981

My beloved Cheryl,

As you see we have arrived here in one piece and all is well! On the trip round we had very rough weather so I feel I passed my first little test. I'm please to say that I've settled in now and life is running fairly smoothly. I'm also pleased to be feeling fairly comfortable in my new position of authority!

It's very lonely without you and I miss you dreadfully. James made a great hit with all on board and is fondly remembered....

All my love, Peter

As Master – La Cordillera

Having gained my Masters (Class 1) Certificate and been given my first Command I had now achieved my main ambition which was to complete the job that I began all those years ago as a Cadet at Warsash. I had no intention of staying at sea forever, but felt I needed more experience in Command so I decided to stick with it until something came up. However, this was a difficult time for Cheryl and me because she was expecting her second baby and I would be away again. Life at sea is hard for the menfolk but infinitely worse for their wives.

La Cordillera, Montreal 17.12.81

My beloved Cheryl,

Every day I have been expecting some news from you and everyday nothing has happened. To tell the truth we struck rough weather near Newfoundland which made writing nearly impossible. Since then we have had snow and fog and a long river passage and I have been rather pre-occupied. However, things have gone well and we arrived without incident.

At the moment the sun is shining and the temperature is about − 5 degrees. In the river there is soft ice floating past. I'm sorry it has been so cold for you in the house but no doubt Mum's heater will help.... All my love, Peter

La Cordillera, Quebec City, 22.12.81

My beloved Cheryl

I must say I had expected something to happen by now! But be patient and don't worry about Doctor R, I'm sure he won't donk you if he has to turn out on Christmas Day. Tell him I have to work Christmas Day as well. I am sure having your Mother around has been a mixed blessing, but I hope you are surviving one way or another.

It's been quite cold and we have a couple of feet of snow on the ground. The river is now completely frozen over and we plough through the ice in good polar style. We have a new Chief Officer who was at Warsash with me and is waiting for his results. Everyone on the ship is expecting a party as a result of your impending labours.

I love you with all my heart, Peter.

La Cordillera, 2.1.82

An unexpected chance to drop you a line from Gibraltar has occurred due to me having to put in and land a sick Second Mate.

The news of little Thomas being born on Christmas Day was wonderful. Please give him my love and of course James too. I hope your weather is not too bad. It has been terrible with us, but ok now. We had quite a good Christmas and a 'rag-bag' fancy dress on New Year's Eve......

All my love, Peter

Cheryl, Peter and Thomas at Christening

The Woods, Charlton Mackrell, 7th January 1982

Beloved Peter,

It seems an age since I wrote to you last – an age of sleepless nights and endless feeding, washing, changing and comforting. Yet in spite of the muddle our two sons are a constant delight to me, and I am impatient for you to come home (even so briefly) to share the pleasures.

I telephoned BM a couple of days ago to enquire when they would know the date of your leave. Mr V. was most pleasant and congratulated us, and said you would be relieved in Spain about the 20th. Well, yesterday when I was upstairs feeding Thomas, there was a knock at the door and when I came downstairs – there was a beautiful arrangement of flowers - from BM. Wasn't that nice of them? It is a triangular shape of yellow daisy like flowers with red-bud roses and London Pride – and is gracing our Drawing Room....

Going to the shops is quite an expedition now. I strap Thomas on me in the Easy Rider and James goes on his reins. Then with Bate on leash in the other hand, we set out. I will be glad of your help when you come home.

I give you my all, body and soul – poor as they are,

Your devoted wife, Cheryl.

La Costa, Port Said, 9.3.1982

My Beloved Cheryl,

Our stay in Greece was spoilt somewhat by being so far from land, and to get ashore was an hour by boat. However, I put a boat service on and most people got to the town. From the ship we could see Eritrea and the little ferries going across the water to the mainland. At least they were visible when it was not pouring with rain.

We have now arrived at the Canal again and I just had to pay the Pilot vessel four thousand cigarettes for his efforts last trip to get us into the convoy despite a late check-in. This time we arrived in time, but it will cost another fourteen cartons, just the normal bribes - quite a lot when you think we go through here about twice a month. This time I hope we stay in the canal and don't take to the fields at full speed like last time and frighten me half to death.

In the meantime, I happened to glance at a post card that one of the sailors was sending home, which read, 'This ship is really cool. I have my own cabin. The Captain thinks he's J.C.! - One finds out a lot about oneself! I had the cook up before me for swearing and carrying on in the galley, and he said they swear worse in monasteries!

All my love, Peter

La Cordillera, Richards Bay, 7.7.1982

My beloved Cheryl,

.... Our stay here has not been too bad at all. I have been taken out to lunch twice, once in Durban and once here. I had very nice food on both occasions. The weather has been good for the most part and the sun shines every day. We have to stop off at Cape Town to pick up some spares, so I may have a chance to write again. Just round here there are signs to beware of crocodiles, but I haven't seen any. The big danger seems to be bandits, who make people very nervous about driving the 80 miles to Durban.

All my love, Pete

So our lives continued along this vein, with three Captains working a rota on two ships, and Cheryl and I still writing copious letters to each other. I was mostly sailing 2 months on and 1 month off. But now I was on the lookout for a shore job, and towards the end of the year I was offered a post as Owners Representative in Jeddah and sent the following Telegram to Cheryl:

OFFERED SHORE JOB JEDDAH GOOD CONDITIONS GB PROVIDE FAMILY ACCOM/TRAVEL/LEAVE PLEASE CONSIDER.

Chapter 4

The next stage

I took the job in Jeddah and flew out on 8th November 1982. The job was Owner's Representative for GB in Jeddah including Saudi Bunkers. Initially overseeing the Management of a fleet of 6 Bulk Carriers, 2 Passenger Vessels, 3 bunker Vessels, 2 Terminal Vessels, and a Bunkering Operation.

Al -Waha Villas Hotel, Jeddah, 8.11.82

My beloved Cheryl,

............I arrived about midnight last night having been met by a little fellow from Al Sabah, and set forth for work at 8 o'clock this morning after a short night. Of course the Managing Director was not here so I took my GB letter to the next chap down. We had a chat and he said they will try to get me a Residents visa as soon as possible, because without it I can't get a Saudi driver's licence or a pass to get either into the Port or the Refinery.

A couple Filipinos also work there and they were detailed to clean out my office and get it ready. The building is in a rather seedy run-down area but my office is very grand in comparison to the others, if a bit tatty. It is large and has air conditioning and a large anti-room affair before you get in. Someone brings tea round fairly frequently. I have a tiddly type-writer.

I'm still totally bemused about the job itself and just staggering along in the dark, even after prolonged discussions which were supposed to make it clear. Anyway by lunch time I was relieved to learn that they all knock off from 1.30 to 5 pm so I came back to the hotel and had a swim. After that 'my driver' took me to the
Photographers to have some shots taken for putting in the multitude of passes I need to go anywhere. After this it seemed a good time to examine what they meant by 'free accommodation' so I asked Mr S and was not comforted by his answer......... Anyway I got back this evening, had a walk, and had dinner, followed by a bottle of WATER. I feel very sober and rather lonely!

All my love as always, Peter

Jeddah 12th November 1982

My beloved Cheryl,

No doubt you will have received my first letter by now written in haste after my first day.

Each morning Mr K – the Al S. Operations Manager picks me up and he is a very nice man and very helpful to me. I am not driving yet because my driver's licence has not been approved, but I am hoping it will be tomorrow. A car is available for me, an enormous white Chevrolet Caprice Classic with white-wall tyres. The traffic here is unbelievable both in behaviour and quantity so how I shall get on I don't know. I have now met the Managing Director Mr Ali G for whom I presumably work although this is by no means clear. He made a speech and then hurried off so I haven't really spoken to him properly. He re-iterated the point about a three month's trial period followed by a one year's contract.

In the meantime, I met a lost Italian man in the hotel who it transpired is also supposed to work for Mr Ali G. He was left to wait five days in the hotel wondering what was going on. However, he may become Technical Superintendent for the Saudi Moon, one of our passenger ships. We visited the accommodation yesterday – I say we because the Italian Mr G will also live there. It comprises a detached block of six flats with a flat roof and an unmade road at the front. There are a few small shops not far away.

Anyway 'our' flat is a huge place with massive rooms and high ceilings with five rooms + kitchen + bathroom + shower room. And of course air conditioning. It is at the top, three stories up. Being on top is a good thing because there is a flat roof surrounded by a high wall and really quite private and safe.

We shall have to strike up some friends with a pool –it is apparently common practice for compounds to allow 'outsiders' in. Added to that the British drive to the beach on Fridays and there is a club at the British Embassy. Ali G expects me to entertain sometimes so we may have some exciting 'dry' parties on our roof.

Our flat, top left

Today I walked a long way and happened upon a Pakistani area and I was quaintly informed it was 7 furlongs long. There were lots of shops with quite high prices but plenty of fruit available. At the moment I feel optimistic and cheerful and the climate, which worried me originally, is perfect. I know it's not July/August, but at the moment, warm dry and very comfortable. Hardly need the air conditioning running.

The work situation is still in chaos. I get 'phone calls from the Port about needing tugs/pilots etc. because of bad weather in the anchorage, and all sorts of things – and I haven't even got a pass to get in yet. Everyone seems to think I'm here to solve all the problems – whatever they are, so I'm learning something new each day......All my love, Peter.

Jeddah 19.11.82

My beloved Cheryl,

Well it's Friday again and so normally a day off except that I went down to the Port and visited Saudi Moon. It's funny having the weekend during the week. I had lunch on-board and saw all the Pilgrims loading up to go back home. All weighed down with an incredible assortment of luggage, refrigerators, TVs, wheelbarrows, bicycles – not to mention all their bedding and cooking equipment. The weather is beautiful and the sea in the harbour is so blue you can hardly believe it.

Jeddah Harbour

Saudi Moon with bunker vessel

On Monday I visited our 'Mother' ship in the anchorage and spoke to the Captain who I knew from old. He is frustrated by the constant muddle. But he originally had the offer of a job ashore and declined it. Now he wants my job! However, Ali G will not hear of it as they don't see eye to eye. On the work front there are a lot of problems and I have written to Ali G and to GB about them. The fact is we are struggling to scrape enough money to operate the Bunker business. I recently discovered that I had a predecessor who stayed two months and then said he must go home to sort things out. He was popular and did a good job, but to the amazement of everyone he was given the sack. This Ali G can be a dangerous and difficult chap and I have no illusions. I fully expected things to be difficult and that was an understatement. I take each day as it comes and everyone keeps telling me to 'watch' someone else! There are many politics and shifting sands, but when I have a small success I quite enjoy it. They didn't need a Captain down here, they needed a gangster!

Cement factory ship in Jeddah

The exchange of letters continues, and elaborates on the delays and difficulties of daily life, getting visas, permits, translations etc. in Saudi. Time drags by with Cheryl and the children waiting to come out, but first I have to get my Iqama before they can start processing her documents. When someone gets their Iqama they are congratulated as if they had just had a baby.

PO box 5650, Jeddah, 10.02.83

My beloved Cheryl,

.........I asked Ali if there was anything I could do to speed things up and he said - No. So with the help of my very nice Sri Lankan friend I am proceeding to do everything myself as best as I can. This involves getting translations of marriage and birth certificates, Master's Certificate, Chamber of Commerce approval, photo-copies of your/my passports, a letter from me, a letter from the company, an application form in Arabic – and some more besides. When all this is assembled they have to be submitted to the Ministry of Foreign affairs. This takes about two weeks and after that there are visits to the Embassy in London to reclaim your passport.

The only bright spot is that I might get a short break and come home on business later this month. The bunkering department is in desperate straits and we have to boost sales, and so I must find a good broker in London to act as our Agent. This is not really my original job here but I am getting to do almost anything, so work here has some interesting days that are full and busy.

All my love, Peter

Shortly after this Cheryl and the children arrived in Jeddah and we spent a few months living in the flat and exploring Arabia at the weekends. Then we all came home on leave in July to cool off.

Exploring the mountains near Taif. It is cooler here and there are some summer palaces in Taif.

Note: By this time, I had been granted my Driving Licence. What a game that is. You have go to the Issuing office armed with a dossier of forms, translations, photographs etc., about 30 pages in total and sit by a large piece of plywood with a hole in it. Then you put your arm through the hole, someone takes blood and you walk out with your new licence!

Camels in the desert

Actually the more you get to know Saudi Arabia and the people, the more fascinating it is. Legend has it that Eve ended her days in Jeddah when she was banished from the Garden of Eden. In Jeddah there is a monument known as 'the Tomb of Eve', to mark her burial place.

The tomb of Eve

Exploring (top picture) and Bedouin village (bottom picture)

Anyway we went on leave and had some discussions and decided that Jeddah was not the right place for us in the long run. And anyway GB was starting to lose their influence and the cement was being carried by vessels owned by Ali G, and GB were ruminating on another job for me anyway.

But I went back to Jeddah on my own to work out my contract. I think Ali G was sorry to see me go. 'We need an honest man here in Jeddah', he said, which was a sort of back-handed compliment.

The bicycle near our house

P.O Box 5650, Jeddah, 2.8.83

My beloved Cheryl,

Things are the same as ever here, possibly worse. Ali has been away in secret to his tribal village for some days. He went without letting anyone know where he was, and left no money to pay staff salaries (including mine). Poor Hussein has almost lost heart. R are pressing for money, P are pressing for money, the Bank are pressing for money, and we are pressing for our salaries and the MD has gone away. Last week the messenger 'lost' a cheque for 1 million US dollars on the way back from the bank, so I don't know what is going on!

I spoke to GB yesterday and they are going to get down to the problem of my future next week when everyone comes back from holiday. They are talking about sending me to the Far East to do with the new liner and feeder service which is being set up there. I love and miss you, Peter

PO box 5650, Jeddah, 5th August 1983

My beloved Cheryl,

I am going to the Bank tomorrow as we have now been paid! Not much news except I went for an explore today about half-way along the inland road from Mecca to Medina. It's about the only road that we didn't go along. There were some interesting wells and date gardens and a wadi with water in it. In the water there were lots of fish and frogs and birds diving in to catch them. This gave way to a high plateau which consisted of a massive lava field of huge stones that was very impressive and much bigger than anything I saw before............

Your loving husband, Peter.

PO Box 5650 Jeddah, 12th August 1983

My beloved Cheryl,

I just finished writing my resignation, so I hope they accept it without a fuss. I am very pleased about the new turn of events. It looks as if I shall go to Bergen for a time before being let loose on S.E. Asia. The work is a combination of Port Captain, Supercargo, Salesman, and Flying Captain all rolled into one.

Most people are drifting back after the summer holidays. I picked up Fahmy and family from the airport today and Ali returned last week. Capt. A. made lunch appointments with my two London contacts then failed to turn up or apologise. What a dirty trick.

Take care my love, Peter.

Moving to Indonesia and (Autumn 1983)

At this time world shipping rates were very depressed and GB decided to start a liner service from Indonesia to USA and Europe based round a hub in Jakarta. The idea being that cargo should be consolidated in Jakarta (as far as possible) by feeder vessel, and then loaded into the large ocean vessels for on-carriage to USA or Europe. And cargo discharged from the ocean vessels should be distributed to Indonesian out-ports in the same way.

Apart from a degree of efficiency offered by this method, it was in many cases the only practical solution because the rivers are too shallow to allow large ships to navigate. Up until this moment all deep sea vessels waited off shore for cargo to come out in barges.

For this purpose, we chartered a small ro-ro/ feeder vessel and modified it for the types of cargo we expected to carry. i.e. Timber, plywood, wood-pulp, etc. And so for the first month I travelled on the feeder vessel endeavouring to get the system set up.

However, I was expected to spend a period of time in Indonesia 'on my own' until we got all this sorted out.

Jakarta 10.11.1983

My beloved Cheryl,

......The good news is that I should be coming to stay in Jakarta in a couple of weeks' time. The work itself is not going too badly and the feeder service appears to be taking roots, or taking off whichever way you look at it.......

Bangkok 20.11.83

.... Well we have come to Bangkok again and this time not so many problems thank goodness. I have left the feeder ship today after a discussion with the office. Little did they know I was on the verge of walking off. Anyway I feel ok now and have had a bath for the first time in a month. They suddenly think I'm going to be frightfully useful elsewhere after all this time so I fly to Singapore tomorrow for a few days and then maybe fly to Borneo for a few more days and then to Jakarta where the resident Mr H is at his wit's end. At least I shall be doing my proper job, and I think they have taken some notice of me now that the feeder thing is running after a fashion.

A dockside market in Bangkok

Yesterday was Loy Krathong, and the ship being parked in the river, we joined the celebration for an hour or so in the evening. We were given these little floats made of frilly paper with candles and joss sticks which have to be lit and floated down the river to the accompaniment of fire-works. I've seen so little of Jakarta having been busy all the time - that I don't know whether it's a good or bad place. The agents in Bangkok are going to drop a hint to GB that I should open an office here – as they seem to approve of me! I must say Thailand is   a super place and I hope we have a chance to see more of it – that is you and I, I mean......

All my love Peter

Philippine Plaza 1.12.83

My beloved Cheryl,

Tomorrow I depart for Davao, and then back to Manila. Everything seems quiet here despite the political troubles but tourism has been affected so there are less people about, apparently. This is rather a super hotel with sports facilities of all kinds. I haven't had a go at anything yet but if you play tennis you not only get a court but two ball boys and an umpire as well.

I had a fairly eventful journey to East Malaysia because all the flights were booked solid and had to take a stand-by from Johore Baru, so I had a 5 a.m. bus ride across the causeway into Malaysia and a long wait.

On arrival at the ship I found a lot of cargo damage due to bad weather and after a night there I came on to the Philippines via Kota Kinabalu and Brunei. East Malaysia is much more modern and organised than one would think and appears to run entirely by Chinese.

I think the Philippines would be a nice place to live as the people are so friendly and helpful. I went to lunch with the agent here and had a successful morning, and a little look round. There is a lot of overt poverty here like in Indonesia....

All my love Peter

Home for Christmas for a short break until 11.1.84

Jakarta 11.1.1984

My beloved Cheryl,

As you see I finally made it to Jakarta - arrived late last night. The fight was quite luxurious by Singapore Airlines as it was a new 747 with us 'executive class' passengers in a special cabin upstairs. However great pain in ears on descending into Arabian waypoint somewhat spoiled the day. However, this soon passed, so I spent a day in Singapore and flew to Sibu the next morning.

Great floods there meant that most of the cargo was cancelled and the ship was anchored nearly seventy miles from the town. Our Agent entertained me most hospitably and after a super Chinese dinner he tried to press me to a young lady for dessert – but I declined his kindness, you'll be glad to know. We went by speed boat to the ship (three hours) and came back by the Gung Fang Express which is a very fast boat service up and down the river.

I asked if there were any dangerous animals in the jungle at the edge of the river and he said no there were not, except someone had recently been 'chilled by a clockodile'.

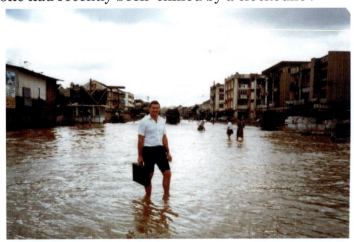

The flight to Kota Kinabalu was by Fokker Friendship. KK is a very nice, modern, prosperous place and Mr L. our Agent took me to lunch and dinner every day, so I have consumed a great deal of prawns, duck, fish etc. all with chop sticks. There is a very nice house on the hill which he says is inhabited by the 'Head of Steak'.

Then I returned to Singapore and had a chat with AK who had just returned from the Philippines and filled me in on his situation – supposedly leaving.

Back in Jakarta I went to the office and found a warm welcome and a brand new desk. I went to the Port and took two Indonesian stevedores to lunch and we had prawns, crab and fish in various dishes. I then went with Mr H. to the place where my visa is being processed and tried to jolly them along a bit. Mr H. knows a house that may be suitable for us and we are going to look at it soon. Realistically we are eyeing end Feb/ early March.

I am having a few days in Jakarta before going forth yet again. Somehow I have to go to Taiwan and Kalimantan at the same time which is impossible.

All love, Peter.

Yokohama, 26.1.84

My beloved Cheryl,

..............We just completed a trans-shipment to Kaohsiung and the people there are very friendly and hospitable. They think I look like JR! I have eaten all sorts of Chinese food and learned a few characters of the writing. They also dragged me out jogging in the park at 7 a.m. one morning which was very interesting, as apart from jogging – or lapsing into a walk in my case – we did some Kung Fu exercise followed by tea and ping-pong at the top of the hill.

Last week-end was a 'good' day according to the lunar calendar and many couples were getting married in the park. I was told that the population is seventy percent Buddhist, fifteen percent Catholic, and fifteen percent Christian! Then we had a drive out in the country and saw the farming which was very interesting. Much eel farming in ponds, rice, bananas, oranges, sugar, sisal, bamboo and many market garden crops. Anyway the inhabitants of the Republic of China have expressed a desire to meet you, and if we ever make it we shall be royally entertained.

Anyway I have come to Japan today to view a candidate vessel to replace our present feeder vessel which is too small. This will be a nice diversion for me, and then on Saturday I go back to Singapore and Jakarta......

Your ever-loving Hull Gee Fung (Lucky Mountain-top)!

Farming in Taiwan

Jakarta 19th Feb 1984

My beloved Cheryl,

I am very conscious of the fact that I haven't written for a while but I will try to explain the situation as clearly as I can.

One reason is that I have been very busy since the beginning of February when I arrived here and have already travelled to Padang and Semarang and we had several ships in port together in Jakarta. It has really been very hectic from early morning until late at night. Yesterday I flew back from Semarang and went straight to the port to inspect another possible new feeder vessel and today is the first day I have had a break since coming back after Christmas.

The other reason is uncertainty in my own mind about the wisdom of coming here at all!! My thoughts are like a confused army with those behind crying forward and those at the front crying back. The truth is I have mixed feelings about Jakarta and don't know what to do.

Leaving aside the school issues, I have decided to buy you a mini-bus (which are about half the price of a car out here) and employ a driver for your own use. This will have to be at 'our' expense but without which things could be a problem for you. I say for 'you' because each day that passes leaves me with the nasty impression that 'I' shall be so occupied elsewhere that 'we' will not be greatly better off than at present.

Anyway to continue. I have looked at several houses and found a very nice one. Full a/c, spacious, 2 servants, 4 bedrooms, modest garden, and very nice. GB says ok and the rent is $1500 per month, payable one year in advance. The house looks nice and secure with wrought iron work over the inside of the windows and plenty of locks etc. The area is not that classy but eighty percent of Jakarta is really a slum and all the stories you hear from Dr Mike R. about it being not such a nice place are frankly true. There is a lot of filth and squalor around but of course the people are desperately poor so you can't blame them. It is a very hard life for the average person here, to the extent that it can be upsetting to witness.........

.... So the problem is that you will be expected to spend a lot of time alone out here and I greatly fear that Jakarta is not a good place to do it.... I don't want the problems of Jakarta to come between us if things turn out badly. On the other hand, it could be super because there is a good side to the place and certain parts of Java are fascinating. There is a lot of colour and bustle and squalor and beauty. It is a super place to visit – but to live here takes a little courage.

So that's the story. I am going inexorably ahead but whether it is wise or right I just don't know. I don't want to let people down or end up without a job because that has problems of its own. I don't even know if I am the right person for this job! .... All love, Peter

Anyway, to cut a long story short Cheryl, James and Tom came out to Jakarta soon after this and we moved into our (new) house

At home in Jakarta

During our time in Jakarta Cheryl's mother came out for a while and they were able to explore some of Java when I was away working, such as the tea plantations at Punchak and also the southern side of Java.

Meanwhile I continued my busy life of travelling round Indonesia and meeting shippers and agents and trying to persuade them to get the cargo ready for each ship. (Not all cargo was moved by feeder vessel). This was not as easy as it sounds because the shippers were always reluctant to get their barges of cargo out to the anchorages, with labour on board, before the ship came. At the same time the ship owner was not happy to wait for the cargo to come out, sometimes a period of 12-24 hours. And sometimes the weather was not good and delayed the operation with a lot of wind and rain and the labour had to live on the barges until the job was done.

So I spent a lot of time going back and forth by speed boat between ship and shore and between islands by light scheduled aircraft...

Me and my gang taking a break

Despite the trials and tribulations of living and working in Indonesia, I must say that it is an amazing place and during my time there I met and worked with some wonderful people. One of the most obvious things that one notices is the amount of sailing vessels still plying for trade. In Jakarta there is a special harbour (Sunda Kelapa) for these and you can see them tied up alongside and working cargo by hand, bag by bag, plank by plank. I later wrote an article about them ....

INDONESIAN BUGIS by Capt. Peter Hull

I am a Master Mariner by profession and former Shipmaster. In 1984 the Shipping Company for which I worked posted me to Indonesia to act as Operations Manager in South East Asia.

Indonesia is a busy, diverse and fascinating country. It is the largest archipelago in the world with over 17,000 islands. It is also one of the most populated. Hence boats have always formed an essential part of life in Indonesia, enabling people to travel and trade between the islands.

Sawing planks by hand

What I normally referred to as Bugis are part of a group of sailing vessels often called Makassar Schooners or Phinisi (sometimes Pinisi). They are probably the last such fleets of sailing boats in the world that still ply for trade. They carry a wide variety of goods such as timber, copra, rice and raw materials to centres like Jakarta, and return to the various river ports throughout the archipelago with material such cement, steel and manufactured items. The main centre in Jakarta is known as Sunda Kelapa, which is the old sailing ship port near Tanjung Priok. It is well worth a visit. It is interesting to see the Bugis being loaded and discharged. Most of the cargo is carried as loose bags or single boards of timber and the stevedores walk up and down a narrow plank carrying a bag of cement, rice, or a couple of planks. The planks of timber are sometimes cut by hand in 'saw pits'. I had been to Indonesia before and seen numerous Bugis at sea under full sail - an impressive and colourful sight.

But my new posting gave me a chance to see one being built in Kota Baru (South Kalimantan). It was rather fortuitous to stumble on this vessel while I was supposed to be doing something else, but it gave me the opportunity to learn a bit about Bugi building. The most interesting thing is that they build the shell first and the frames second.

Here is an extract from an article about them……

'Pinisi have always been assembled using wooden pegs to join the timbers. We would call the fasteners "trunnels" or tree nails.

The sequence of assembly is different than we in the West would ordinarily assume. First the keel is laid, then the stem and stern post are erected, as usual. Then, however, rather than setting up the whole array of the hull shell. The frames are pegged to the planks, to the keel, and to each other where the frame segments are joined. The frame butt ends either lap across the keel (Sulawesi style), or are joined to a floor member (more common in Kalimantan), depending on the tradition from which the individual boat builders have come.

This "planking first" approach may seem odd to our rigidly defined approach to shaping a ship in the West, but this is as the builders among the Indonesian islands have done it since no one knows when. This is very much the most common method used throughout Indonesian, Malaysian, and other South and Southeast Asian waters, and the method has served the people very well indeed'.

(I think the ancient Greeks used to build trireme this way)

Suffice it to say that building a Bugi requires a lot of skill and experience. They are impressively large and built by hand using village labour without the help of power tools. (There are quite a lot of websites showing Pinisi building).

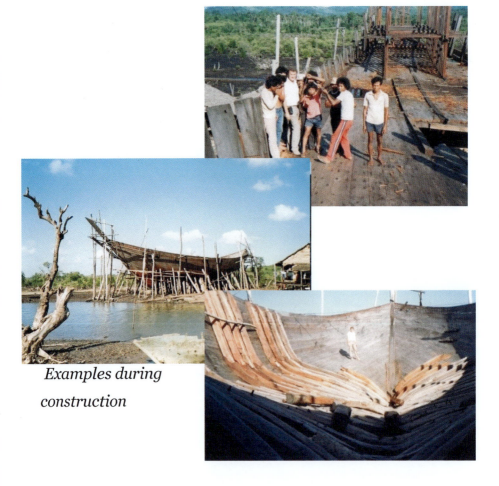

Examples during construction

Sunda Kelapa

Suffice it to say we had some good times in Jakarta. Cheryl and I made some life-long friends and we talked about our time there for many years afterwards. But it was very hard for us. So much time spent travelling for me and such long periods alone for Cheryl. In the end we reluctantly decided enough was enough and at the end of my contract we came home to Somerset.

Rural scenes from Kalimantan

Chapter 5

The Last Phase

So after about a year and a half in Indonesia, we came home to Somerset and GB gave me the job of Owner's Representative (UK) at Portbury, near Bristol. As we lived not far away, this was an excellent opportunity to have a more normal and settled home life. I was to look after the company's interests, attend their vessels, and attend to their customers' needs and so on in the UK. The customers were mostly industrial corporations, paper mills, timber companies etc. We had inbound services mainly from Canada, Brazil, Chile and South Africa. We also had some export cargo, from Sheerness and Dublin.

As the Company grew our life became busier. I started on my own at Bristol but a few years later we had an office of five people, two Port Captains, two support staff and me. We had a lot going on as the ships often called at several ports and we had to work them round the coast on the tides. Most Ports in UK are tide restricted and so we endeavoured to complete cargo operations in one port, and sail on or near high water, and then catch the tide again at the next port – thereby keeping lost time to a minimum. Apart from the UK and Ireland I also occasionally covered some other ports in Europe, e.g. Rotterdam and Antwerp. All this involved some travelling, but not for long periods.

Having missed the births of James and Tom when I was at sea, I was able to be present when Rosalind was born on 31.1.86. It was intended that she should be born at home, but Dr R was slightly worried and insisted that she should be in hospital, at least for the birth. When the time came, and Cheryl was in labour I rushed her into Yeovil hospital and Rosalind was born soon afterwards. They were allowed home later that day.

Meanwhile, apart from children, Cheryl was beginning to take an interest in sheep and started up what was to become 'The Hullswood Flock of Pedigree Jacob Sheep'. Being an 'old farm boy' this was something I could help her with and an interest that we could share. She started with a few sheep and rented some small paddocks in the village – later growing to 30 or 40 ewes. There was another sheep farmer in the village who used to help occasionally at such times as 'dipping' because he had his own sheep dip. If you have a few sheep you need all sorts of other equipment such as hurdles, tractors and trailers to take animals to shows and/or market and to fetch hay and so forth.

Rosalind

William

Cheryl at show with sheep

In the early days we used to show quite a lot. There is a fair amount of work involved in showing, in getting the sheep tame enough to be led on a halter, and also the presentation of the animals requires a lot of attention to detail such as shampooing, oiling hooves and horns etc.

A couple of sheep trailers that I built at home.

And then on 20.07.1989 William was born at home in Charlton Mackrell.

Rosalind on my (pride and joy), our T20 Ferguson Tractor

And so our family was now complete with a total of five children, four of whom lived with Cheryl and I, and Rebecca who lived with her mother in Sussex. And so we had a busy life with children, work and sheep. We had a lot of help from Maria in particular, who did the school run for us, because Cheryl did not drive and I was at work during the week.

We also had a problem. Our house was too small for six people, so we embarked on our own 'Grand Design'. We decided to add a couple of additional bedrooms onto the house. As we couldn't find a builder who could do it in time, or within reasonable cost, we decided to do it ourselves and employ sub-contract labour.

The Woods Extension

We had an architect and he eventually secured planning approval for an extension in the form of a T. with two additional bedrooms and two additional bathrooms, one up and one down. As our house was a listed building any alterations had to be in keeping with the old. So the roof had to be thatched and the windows had to be bespoke, and the construction had to be of blue lias stone from the quarry in the village. Our thatcher had records of thatching the house for the last 120 years, but when we broke open the roof space to admit the new roof timbers our architect was certain that the house dated back seven or eight hundred years and was in fact an old 'Hall House'.

And then disaster struck! The following year I was away in Tilbury with some visitors from abroad when late at night the telephone rang and it was Cheryl calling. 'Our house has been flooded', she said, and went on to explain how she heard a noise outside and went to investigate. She opened the door and water gushed in. James managed to snatch William and head upstairs and Cheryl called for help into the darkness. Fortunately, the neighbours heard her calls and took them all into their house for the night. Our house was completely blacked out with water in the electrics. So I called my Dad and I arrived home at first light, and he a little later. The initial plan was that he would take Cheryl and the children back home with him.

Anyway, I immediately went into town and hired a portable petrol driven pump. When I arrived back I fixed up the pump and started pumping and went to have a look at the cause of all this mayhem. We had a small stream running through and around our garden and it appeared that the branch of a tree and other debris had created a dam just upstream. After heavy rain the stream had become blocked and diverted itself through the field behind our house and into the garden. The water was now about one-metre-deep throughout the house.

Everything below this level was destroyed by the dark muddy water. I called the Insurance Company who explained that we should get all the carpets and damaged items out of the house. Wet carpets are really heavy! Anyway, as I had cleared the 'dam' no more water was coming in and the levels were receding as we pumped and things started to look a bit better. It was nearly Christmas but fortunately most of the presents that we had bought were unaffected.

In the end Cheryl and the children decided to remain at home and we dragged all the damaged stuff out into the garden and got the electrics back up and running. Despite having a dehumidifier going for about three months it took absolutely ages to get straight. Some furniture was taken away to be refurbished, and we lost a lot a books from the bottom shelves, never to be replaced. Fortunately, the Insurance Company paid up, but we never felt secure again. Although we put in some flood prevention measures and never suffered such a catastrophic event again. The main difficulty was that whenever we thought we might like to move, potential buyers got wind of the fact that the house had flooded and they took fright. So whether we liked it or not we were stuck there. Later on this did cause some difficulty, but eventually after about ten years the episode was forgotten by everyone, except by us.

Meanwhile work continued to go well. Apart from just dealing with UK matters I became increasingly involved with the business of shipping and travelled to a number of places to visit my 'opposite numbers' and to meet the shippers, and see the factories, mills, plantations etc. So in particular I travelled to Brazil, Chile and British Colombia, sometimes with managers of the UK Port Industry and sometimes alone.

Scenes from Chile and Brazil

Cheryl was also the local organiser for UNICEF, and during our time at Charlton Mackrell she raised a lot of money. She was involved in producing a Cantata for Bosnia in which Rosalind performed. She also organised several garden parties in our garden in aid of UNICEF.

27.1.96

LANC

Local News ———————— **Newsdesk: 01935 74551 – Fax: 01935 26963**

● IN TUNE: Children from the Charltons were among those taking part in a concert in aid of UNICEF at Charlton Mackrell community centre on Saturday. More than £900 has been raised so far for the children's charity, which celebrates its 50th anniversary this year. *Picture by Clive Davies.*

About this time my Company decided to move the Head Office from Norway to Esher in Surrey, so my office was incorporated in the new set up and I was given a new role, more to do with improving the performance of the fleet which had grown to about 60 vessels from the mere 16 when I joined.

The new Head Office

I became Senior Ops Manager and part of an Operations Desk where we dealt with all the many things that crop up every day in the life of a busy Shipping Company. It also implied crew training and we started to run familiarisation course in Manila for Filipino Officers.

In Manila

All continued to go well but when I was offered the chance of another job nearer home (Bristol) I took it. We only have one life. Although after such a long time with one company I was somewhat reluctant to leave, I felt I had reached a sort of plateau. Everyone was very understanding and said they were sorry to see me go. The last twenty years, beginning from when I was a Chief Officer on La Cordillera to Senior Operations Manager had been a very creative time for me and I met and worked with some wonderful people, clever, hard-working and dedicated. They gave me a small brass plaque when I left that says, PETER - WORK, WORK, WORK! - Well I did my best!

I shall fast-forward to the millennium year 2000. Almost every year for the past twenty years we had our family holidays in France and Cheryl and I liked the country very much and could see the advantages of living there, so we started to look around to see if this might be possible. We went out in 1999 and drew a blank, but in the spring of 2000 we found a possibility – a small farm in Aquitaine. I think we both very much wanted to 'break out' and do something for ourselves before it was too late and we were too old and too set in our ways. So we decided to throw caution to the wind and go for it. James and Tom were off to University so we just had to think about Rosalind and William. Cheryl also had one eye on her sheep, and the idea of having a small farm with all the animals on hand, rather than grazing away from home was a very attractive one.

So to cut a long story short, we sold our house, I gave up my job and we bought Laudonie, near Teyjat, an 18th century farm house and buildings set in about 15 acres of ground, in the most beautiful hills of the Dordogne. It was in a bit of a mess; I have to admit. The fields were partly overgrown and the house needed a lot of attention. But we were not deterred. We took almost everything with us – furniture, dogs, cat, ducks etc., and the sheep came by livestock truck the following day. Actually the livestock lorry got stuck on the little bridge just down the road in Teyjat! But they got it off.

This was the start of a big adventure for us and I bought a new tractor and set about clearing the fields and building a new sheep shed just behind one of the existing sheds. One of the most amazing things, that bowls me over even today when I remember it, is the smell of the hay. During the first winter we had to buy in hay and a load of large round bales arrived. When I opened the first one there was an absolute explosion of perfume from all the flowers, herbs and grasses locked up in the hay.

We also did a lot of work on the house which was, to some extent assisted by an accident. It had been a bitterly cold day and we lit the fire early. (We had a lot of oak cord wood, about a metre long which gave off a good heat and also heated one or two radiators). Suddenly the 'phone rang, 'Vous avez un feu dans votre chiminee' said a voice, and sure enough we had a chimney fire. So we called the Pompiers who took their time but eventually arrived. After the normal pleasantries and kisses they got down to it and put the fire out. But not before quite a lot of damage had been done which required a new chimney and some new ceilings. After that we installed a new kitchen and looked very smart. Normally the weather in the summer was fairly hot, sometimes very hot, but the winters it can be very cold. One winter our pipes froze up completely.

Most French villages have a spring (source) where people used to do their washing, and we had one about a mile away. In the summer I used to go there with the tractor and fill up drums of this exquisite water for the sheep. We actually had two houses, our large farm house and an older small one just a few metres away that we called 'Maison des Amis'. Under the 'Maison des Amis' was a cistern into which all the rain gutters led, so that you could store water in the winter in readiness for the dry summers. It was completely dark to prevent organic growth and the size of a small swimming pool.

The local town of Javerhlac was a couple of miles away and you can get most things there. They had a butcher, baker, grocers, post office, doctor, garage etc. We found all the people both friendly and helpful. The really nice thing about France is the fresh bread and also the polite way country people behave in shops. We had a number of friends both English and French. One of our best friends had a large house that they shared with a French family and in the grounds they had a small golf course and a swimming pool. So we spent a fair amount of time there and our children loved the pool, the water for which was pumped from their source.

Some views of Laudonie, front, back and inside

Although it wasn't planned, after a while I thought I ought to try and earn some money. As luck would have it one of my old colleagues called me up about some temporary work in South East Asia where his Company was taking over another Company and they needed someone to help with the changeover. So I found myself back in my old haunts of Jakarta and Indonesia for a few weeks. This occasional work suited me rather well, and began to grow into something quite useful. Another former colleague asked me to go to the Middle East so I was soon back in Jeddah again! But look as I might I could not find the tomb of Eve! It was both instructive and a pleasure to go back to these places after quite a long absence. Not a great deal had changed and I was pleased to find that my knowledge and experience of the region was of some use.

After we had been in France a couple of years I was diagnosed with prostate cancer and had go into hospital for an operation. Although I recovered from the operation, the cancer was not fully cured. I think when something like this happens you are never quite the same again. This made me worry about our future and worry about how long we could sustain our life in France. Anyhow we soldiered on but for various reasons, we had sent both our youngest children back in schools in England.

After about four years in France we took the decision to sell up and return to the UK, to be nearer the family as a whole. It took a while to sell, but when it did we bought a house in Langport to be closer to the children.

We had hardly settled into Arlington House, Langport, when I went down with Sepsis and Toxic Shock and had be rushed into ITU. So began a series of treatments and operations lasting three and a half years in total (22 weeks actually in hospital). Mercifully I survived but it left me a bit wonky and needing to walk with a stick.

Nevertheless, a bit later we managed a cruise down the Nile and that was a wonderful experience. And we saw all the sights and enjoyed beautiful weather.

Then in about 2010 I was well enough to buy a boat of my own. This was something I had always wanted to do and I found one for sale at Topsham. It was a 22-foot sloop built in the 1960's of oak and mahogany. I kept it on the River Exe in the summer, and on a farm near Langport in the winter. We got a lot of fun out of it and named it ANNE after my mother.

Postscript

I often wonder whether going to France was a good or bad thing. It certainly wasn't a wise decision, but who wants to be wise when you can have a last hurrah. I could have taken the easy route and cruised into retirement working at Bristol. Only another five years to go, plod, plod. But I didn't want the year 2000 to be the year we 'nearly' went to France. Cheryl and I were always hard working and creative people and I think we were more proud of going to France than anything else we did, because we did it ourselves. All the planning, and taking our Noah's Ark with us. And despite everything we loved it there, having our own space and independence. We bought more land and improved the house and garden. We should probably have done it years before and in a bigger way, but we couldn't have afforded it then.

I think a combination of my illness and the disappointment of leaving France may have contributed to Cheryl becoming unwell and she passed away on 3.2.2016.

My wonderful family

After Cheryl died I have been busy composing several books. Latterly I was 'found' by Christine who I mentioned at the start of these memoirs. I've not seen her for 52 years and she is now a widow and lives in County Durham, but we get along fine, we have taken up where we left off, and now have a good loving relationship.

Christine and I at a Bedford School reunion.